THE
SECRETS
OF THE
SEASONS

Praise for *The Secrets of the Seasons*

"A thought-provoking and timely reminder from the Shaman of Wall Street of why we are all here. If you have the courage to read it, this book will change your world."

—Richard Barrett, Managing Director of the
Academy for the Advancement of Human Values

"An amazing book about waking up—in the very deepest sense—written by a man who has mastered the ways of Wall Street and the secrets of the shaman's journey. His story is all of our stories, from the dark night of the soul to the inner fire of certainty that life has real purpose and that the world needs our gift."

—Judy Rodgers, International Projects,
The Brahma Kumaris, Founder, Images & Voices of Hope

"Lawrence Ford's book is a poignant reminder that we all have a divine purpose and reason for being here. It is a gift of a lifetime of hard-won insight and wisdom that is grounded in the courageous vulnerability of a beautiful, perceptive, and compassionate being. His only desire is to assist us (the reader) on our own personal pilgrimage through life's seasons to manifest our unique destiny."

—Will Kennedy, Senior Program Officer, United Nations

"Perhaps the most unique person straddling the worlds of investing and spirituality, Lawrence Ford has given us a unique and singularly valuable gift. Bravely drawing on his own extraordinary life experiences, Lawrence has distilled timeless wisdom down to its actionable essence. Like all works of mastery, this book arrives at the 'simplicity on the other side of complexity.' *The Secrets of the Seasons* is destined to become a modern classic of spiritual teaching in the tradition of *The Prophet*, *The Untethered Soul*, and *The Alchemist*."

—Raj Sisodia, Cofounder of the Conscious Capitalism movement, coauthor, *The Healing Organization: Awakening the Conscience of Business to Help Save the World* and *Everybody Matters: The Extraordinary Power of Caring for Your People Like Family*

"In this book Lawrence Ford boldly transcends the trivial conversations surrounding leadership and success. He invites us to traverse unseen worlds by magnifying the magic that it is to be alive. This is a MUST-READ for anyone who is deeply interested in manifesting his or her greatest gifts on earth, for it reminds us that behind the veil of perception, there is a reality waiting to be encountered. Beautifully written, accessible, and straight from the heart—his words will find homes for themselves in the places in you that matter most."

—Srini Pillay, MD, Harvard-trained psychiatrist, brain researcher, technology entrepreneur, and author, *Tinker Dabble Doodle Try: Unlock the Power of the Unfocused Mind*

"An old proverb says, 'To be fully human, we must make room within ourselves for the Universe to enter.' Through the story of his own awakening, Lawrence Ford powerfully illustrates why it's critical that we become fully human—for our own sakes, and for the urgent sake of changing the collective dream we're in—while also illuminating how, through a balance of ancient wisdom, modern thought, and personal insight. A timely and authentic read."

—Claudia Welss, Chairman, Institute of Noetic Sciences, and Chair, Invest in Yourself at NEXUS Global

"What a timely read! In an age of much disruption being grounded in the knowingness that we are here for a reason gives so much hope. Lawrence's thrilling sharing of his own journey coupled with a framework for us to follow gives a pathway for each and every one to follow. Thank you, Lawrence, for writing your journey and for your intuitive and analytical gifts to share with us in such a catching way."

—Kristin Engvig, Founder Women's International Network & WIN Conference

"It is true. There are seasons to each of our lives. What we lack today is a tradition of elders we allow to elder us. Lawrence is one. He does it mainly by telling his story, especially of his awakening into the Third Season most of us in our modern societies do not even know exists."

—Terry Mollner, a Founder of Calvert Social Funds, author, *Our Mutual Blind Spot Since Our Invention of Words*

"*The Secrets of the Seasons* is a book of its time. Lawrence has made this book personal, while at the same time giving us the steps that can help us cultivate our uniqueness. There is an awakening across this planet, and this book lights the fire of possibility that lives within. Let the journey begin!"

—Jyoti Ma, Grandmother Vision Keeper of The Fountain

"*The Secrets of the Seasons* is about transformations in spirit and life. It is a compelling personal account as well as about spiritual development and guiding the crises in life that inevitably arise and, if mastered, awaken innate human processes to be a more compassionate, caring, and successful person. A road map to realize our true being and destiny of the soul in contemporary culture."

—Larry Peters, PhD, anthropologist and author,
Tibetan Shamanism: Ecstasy and Healing

"In reading *The Secrets of the Seasons*, you may get a feeling, deep within your soul, that you've been given an opportunity at just the right time, at exactly the right moment of your life, for you to begin a journey of much-needed self-realization, self-discovery, and magic. Lawrence Ford's experience, spiritual wisdom, and his passion for sharing this gift with the world make this spiritual journey accessible to everyone, no matter the spiritual path, life experience, or current life stage of the reader.

"This book will help you reconnect with who you really are, with the universe and its wisdom, and with the magic inherent in all of existence. With his keen insights, helpful practices, and respect for the wisdom of ancient traditions, Lawrence invites all of us to rediscover ourselves and how we are all connected to each other and to all of the natural world."

—Kurian Thomas, Vice President,
Spiritual Transformation, Fetzer Institute

"Lawrence has developed a profound model of spiritual growth through four seasons of life, bringing the reader to a real personal waking and then into living whole. In *The Secrets of the Seasons*, we learn why Lawrence does the highly popular leadership programs for which he is renowned. We learn of his journey as a visionary shamanic soul formally trained with some of the finest shamans and healers in Nepal and elsewhere.

"This book is eminently practical in its presentation of easily understood meditational techniques and spiritual exercises from which we can all benefit. He weaves into this journey his career path as a wealth management advisor who consistently approaches his clients with kindness and love.

"May all those on Wall Street become such shamans. He reminds me of the Wall Street investor Sir John Templeton, known as 'the Tennessee mystic,' who succeeded with the spiritual wisdom, honesty, service, and love for which he was so well respected. Were Sir John still with us, I would want to introduce him to Lawrence and listen in with an energized smile."

—Stephen G. Post, PhD, Founding Director, Center for Medical Humanities, Compassionate Care & Bioethics, School of Medicine, Stony Brook University; President, Institute for Research on Unlimited Love (www.unlimitedloveinstitute.org); author, *Why Good Things Happen to Good People: How to Live a Happier, Healthier, and Longer Life through the Simple Act of Giving* and *Love on Route 80: The Hidden Mystery of Human Connectedness*

"In *The Secrets of the Seasons*, Lawrence Ford skillfully weaves his own experience as an investor with the questions that challenge each of us: How do we connect more fully with ourselves and community? How do we navigate questions of capital and wealth management with meaning and purpose? By presenting us with reflections on his own journey, Lawrence helps us explore our experience of the seasons as we move through and as we address the paths we take in our lives. Just a pleasure to read and a great contribution in these challenging times."

—Jed Emerson, author, *Purpose of Capital: Elements of Impact, Financial Flows and Natural Being*

"Lawrence Ford's extraordinary life story, his financial expertise, and shamanic wisdom—it all contributes to his unique way of being and living whole. He is the healing bridge between two worlds: business and spirituality. He enables others to make a positive difference in the world with the power of money by adding consciousness to finance, by creating and holding a space for purpose: You're Here for a Reason. *The Secrets of the Seasons* includes a genius Soul System Operating Map: the perfect vaccine for personal flourishing and collective thriving in a post-COVID world."

—Patrik Somers, Founder of Evolution Inside Out and facilitator coach and partner of Barrett Values Centre

"*You can't do it like this anymore*—In his book *The Secrets of the Seasons*, Lawrence Ford recounts this call to awaken. A clanging bell heard by most of us who try to listen to our circumstance at one point or another in our lives. *You can't do it like this anymore*—it's the movie in my head that I watch as metaphor over and over at moments of necessary change: There I was, the founder of a cardiovascular disease prevention and rehab program at a major university hospital in New York, sitting in the nursing station, doing my charting, and smoking a cigarette. The incongruity is of the head shaking variety— and yet there it is—a rut, of sorts, the kind we get into when we lose track of ourselves and yield to the rut. We are each here for a reason, and Lawrence Ford's book shows us a path to our remembering ourselves and that purpose. Opening up to his teachings and listening to our own soul is a first step."

—S. Robert Levine, MD

"*The Secrets of the Seasons* is a guidebook for those who find themselves 'walking between worlds.' Those who know deep in their heart and soul there are other dimensions of reality, who experience signs or unexplainable phenomena yet live and work in the everyday world. Perhaps feeling their daily life is a pantomime compared to the hidden dimensions that are just out of reach. If this describes you, or if this intrigues you, then this book is for you, written by a shaman who fluidly passes between the worlds of finance, business, and transdimensional consciousness. Lawrence lights the way by sharing his unique story, providing a path to recognize your purpose and to become fully expressed as the uniquely extraordinary gift to the world you were born to share."

—Patricia Klauer, chiropractor,
Data Strategy Consultant, World-Walker

"Lawrence Ford, for the first time, discloses his fascinating personal quest exploring the Yin and the Yang of both Wall Street's asset management practice *and* Himalayan shamanism. A recommended read for everyone who subscribes to the idea that a change in perspectives is worth 80 IQ points and for those who aspire to stay relevant in our challenging times."

—Björn Larsson, CEO, The ForeSight Group, coauthor, *The Rise of the Meaningful Economy & Changing the World We Create*

"A courageous, personal testament to the importance of recognizing the higher purposes we choose to guide our lives. Our globalized connectivity has brought us together in real time and demands our full attention and global cooperation. Whatever the self-inflicted crises cognitively challenged humans have created, from pandemics to the climate crisis, our planet is now our programmed learning environment, teaching us directly. The lesson: expanding our awareness and becoming fully conscious of all our ethical imperatives for our common future."

—Hazel Henderson, FRSA, author, *Mapping the Global Transition to the Solar Age* and other books, CEO, Ethical Markets Media

"What you hold in your hands is a true gem from a shaman, a leader, and a visionary. To make it through these evolutionary times we need visionaries like Lawrence who can help us bridge business and spirituality, capital, and magic. We are not human beings having a mechanistic experience, but spiritual beings having divinely human ones. To have the most fulfilling, happy, and abundant lives, we need to embrace our true authentic self—wholly spiritual, wholly physical, and abundant in every way. Lawrence's spiritual, financial, and personal handbook helps us handle the most interesting times humanity has ever been called to face."

—Michael Sandler, Host of the Inspire Nation Show, www.InspireNationShow.com

"Lawrence Ford's new book *The Secrets of the Seasons* has arrived at a very timely inflection point. We are all isolated from our old 'normal' in which we had taken so much for granted, served what we now clearly see were the wrong priorities, and started petrifying in a creeping global indifference, anaesthetized to the plight of others, which was reaching depths so dizzying that we had given up on trying to deal with them. Luckily, we have writers, thinkers, and caring fellow spirits who speak truth and keep the flame of purpose and caring alive. Enter Lawrence Ford and his new book *The Secrets of the Seasons*. If enough of us reflect on these issues and then take the further step of recalibrating our priorities and values, realizing, as Lawrence has, that it *is* after all possible to move the mountains that keep us from the kind of compassionate new humanism that will restore humankind's dignity, and that we can still avert catastrophic consequences."

—Leslee Udwin, Founder and President, Think Equal

"Aikido founder Morihei Ueshiba stated: 'Every master, regardless of the era or the place, heard the call and attained harmony with heaven and earth.' He adds, 'There are many paths leading to the top of Mount Fuji, but there is only one summit—Love.' In this compelling, open-hearted and masterful work, Lawrence Ford guides us to attain harmony between our highest aspirations (Heaven) and the reality of our everyday lives (Earth). Wherever you are in your ascent, and whatever path you are on, Ford's profound stories will inspire and energize every step you take. Infused with loving consciousness, *The Secrets of the Seasons* serves as a spiritual compass directing us toward the summit of our own fulfillment."

—Michael J. Gelb, Aikido 5th dan and author,
How to Think Like Leonardo da Vinci

"Lawrence is like this in real life. He embodies the reconciliation of the acceptance of the world as it is, the will and ambition to change it for good and the desire to be successful in a competitive commercial world. He has arrived at a place where he sees and finds meaning from life and its unfolding, painful as it is sometimes, and yet at every stage seeks to make conscious choices and live life the way he wishes with the faith that it is all as it is meant to be. This is his story and offers some beautiful lessons."

—Ketan Patel, CEO, Greater Pacific Capital, author, *The Master Strategist*

"Larry Ford is an extraordinary thinker and this succinct, well-written book will help people lead deeper, more fulfilling lives."

—Gene Stone, author, *Forks Over Knives*

"*The Secrets of the Seasons* carries a deeply inspiring and precious message of wisdom relevant to all of us at every moment of our lives, not only in the darkest moments but even in the brightest. Life is our partner and complement in the spiritual evolution of humanity, a mirror which provides by reflection the progressive knowledge we need for self-discovery and self-realization. Life brings us precisely what we need to awaken our consciousness for further progress and the capacity to calmly, patiently, and cheerfully learn from our experiences without self-justification or regret is indeed a secret for continuous spiritual progress."

—Garry Jacobs, President and CEO, World Academy of Art & Science; Chairman of the Board and CEO, World University Consortium; Vice President, The Mother's Service Society, India

"Lawrence has brought timeless wisdom and practices into a modern setting with grace, good humor, and excellent personal examples. That this compelling guide to a better personal and collective future emerges from the heart of the financial industry makes me hopeful indeed! A must-read for the modern change agent."

—Tim Kelley, Certified Conscious Capitalism Consultant and author, *True Purpose*

"In my daily work, shamans never came to my mind, that is, until I met Lawrence Ford. His book comes out as half of humanity is under confinement, and we face the worst health and economic crisis of our lifetime. We awake to the realization that we are all interconnected and need borderless solidarity. We are all asking ourselves what can I, individually and collectively, do? In his 'You are here for a reason,' Lawrence uses his personal (painful) journey and shaman initiation to offer us tools and concepts to help guide us to use our unique gifts to support ourselves, each other, and our communities to rebuild more equal, inclusive, and sustainable economies."

—Chantal-Line Carpentier, Chief, UNCTAD New York Office of the Secretary General (United Nations)

THE SECRETS OF THE SEASONS

YOU'RE HERE FOR A REASON

LAWRENCE FORD

Medical disclaimer: The information contained in this book is not intended as a substitute for the advice and/or medical care of the reader's physician or mental health provider, nor is it meant to discourage or dissuade the reader from seeking the advice of his or her healthcare professionals. If the reader has any questions concerning the information presented in this book, or its application to his or her particular medical profile, he or she should consult his or her physician. Neither the authors nor the publisher shall be liable or responsible for any loss or damage allegedly arising as a consequence of the reader's use or application of any information or suggestions in this book. This book reflects the individual views and opinions of Lawrence Ford.

Production team: Sandra Wendel, Write On, Inc., editor; Teddi Black, cover design; Ben McLean, McLean Audio, audiobook production; Megan McCullough, interior design.

ISBN: 978-1-7348449-0-0 (paperback)
ISBN: 978-1-7348449-1-7 (ebook)
ISBN: 978-1-7348449-2-4 (audiobook)

Published by
Conscious Capital Press
Website: www.LawrenceFord.org
Email: info@LawrenceFord.org

Cover photo by Lawrence Ford. See the following section for the story behind the photo.

About the Cover Photo

I took this photo on top of a sacred mountain in Montserrat, Spain, in February 2020. On that day the single bell at 4:30 a.m. called for meditation. Then more bells rang out at the prescribed time and tempo.

I was at the home of the Black Madonna, a site where millions had made the pilgrimage since the 1500s. I was there with my family by irrational grace.

The clouds cascaded over the mountains while the ominous sounds of owls and unnamed, unseen night creatures called from below. For the next hour I stood in a semi-meditative state thinking about how many years this entire scene has, and will, continue to play out, over and over without interruption. Then the deafening clanging of the bells rang out like an encore at the end of a fireworks display. The sky turned pink and orange while chants of monks and day creatures beckoned the pilgrims to another day of worship.

The prior evening, from that very location, after many, many long nights of writing, I had sent this manuscript to my editor. It was time.

Unbeknownst to any of us, it was the eve of the global coronavirus pandemic—a virus that was about to wipe out so many lives from Spain on its way to America, and eventually the rest of the world. I was standing above the clouds in pure bliss, but inside I had a mysterious haunting, hollow feeling I could not understand.

As I sit in my home with my family now, in monotonous mandated isolation, I wonder if the bells still ring. Our mother has given us all a time-out to go to our respective corners to think about what we have done. I pray this book will help us hear the call of this global third season of waking to remind us that we are all here for a reason and everything matters.

Contents

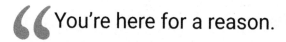
You're here for a reason.

One day we will realize that there is nothing more important in the world than knowing that each of us has a gift and that we are all here to support each other to fulfill that gift.

Introduction: You're Here for a Reason

There is a purpose to life. Find the light inside you ... feed it, fire it up, and let it shine with abandon throughout the world. It will reflect upon you in ways unimagined.

Good *can* triumph over evil when healthy imaginal cells—awakened human beings who have discovered each other—come together and use their collective energy and intelligence to overturn the current dystopian dream we find ourselves locked into, a dream on track to self-destruct and greatly harm our species and the earth.

The Secrets of the Seasons can help a sleepwalking world awaken and live a life of passion, purpose, and magic. There is an ancient yet easily testable way of bringing love and joy back into the world. We can use it to come together and shake people from their slumber while initiating a new paradigm of consciousness and capitalism, loving respect, and a better life for all.

By embodying the deep meaning and transformative potential these secrets have for all of our lives, and by learning to make use of the upgraded big picture reality co-creation operating system that underlies this set of ancient wisdom-based roadmaps, we can come to live whole, in peace and prosperity, individually and collectively, as ourselves, our families, and the whole world.

When embraced and understood, the power and simplicity of these secrets—as given to me and as shared with you as best I can in this book—will transform your life.

You're Here for a Reason

Like every snowflake, the special song your soul sings is completely unique to you, just as your reason for being here is unique to you. Throughout the entirety of our physical existence on earth—through all the twists and turns on all the pathways that each of us goes down as we move through the cyclical seasons of our lives—we are guided to remember our soul's unique song and our reason for being here. You can tune into that knowledge at any moment of your life—including right now—just as you can tune into the pure love you knew yourself to be upon being born and for quite some time after that.

The wonders, the miracles, the awe, the illimitable beauty of existence itself—these gifts are all real, eternal, and always yours for the taking in any micro-moment. Similarly, if you were to, for even one moment, seriously and thoroughly consider the complexity (and speed!) of the chemical reactions going on within each of your body's 75 trillion (or so) cells every single second, you would likely be bowled over with gratitude for how much is already always being done for you through every single cycle of your breath.

And think of the odds that brought you right here and right now to this very moment. How much had to happen just perfectly to have created you? Let's say the odds are 1 in 700 trillion against you—just as you are—being born at all. Well, the odds of the miracle of consciousness that is you reading these words at this moment is a number far beyond imagination.

But it's easy to forget all this. The times we live in are interesting but chaotic and seemingly senseless, with many people entirely abandoning the notion of the soul, no less an intelligent, beneficent universe sending signs and signals every moment to remind us of why, personally, we are here, and how to most effectively embrace our personal *raison d'être*.

Put differently, far too many of us have forgotten not just *why* we're here, but the very nature of our own being—who and what we are in the first place. This soul challenge is not our sole challenge, but it is a good place to begin our first introductory tour through the seasons.

Challenges and Opportunities: Here for a Reason through Every Season

In the first season of life—the season of being—each of us is born knowing that we are a pure soul. Then comes the doing of the second season, where we each undertake the life before us. Then we have no choice but to begin practicing the alignment of that second season doing with our first season being. But attempting to sync up our lives with a world that so often seems to have gone crazy is not easy. Not easy at all. Almost everyone experiences many good and beautiful moments during the second season of their lives, but in the end, far too many of us fall—and stay—asleep.

If we are pressured to only believe in the things we have been taught or seen, the magic and purpose of life is stripped from our world as we become angry, sick, numb, and depressed. So many people believe life no longer matters. Our experience becomes a monotonous monochrome nightmare, joyless and stifling, punctuated by occasional doses of fun, diversion, and pleasure.

Slipping into ruts, we can become consumed with survival, negative news, and petty drama. We can become automatons with no real purpose or destination, desperately hoping something will change, but never actually doing anything about it. The broader world often seems even worse, with so many people and organizations—often in positions of high power and trust—dysfunctionally acting out their frustrations and tensions on others. Communities, nations, and the whole world suffer terribly, and there often seems little we can do about it.

But then, through what can be rightly held as a miracle or moment of grace, at some point in our lives, each and every one of us is gifted with a third season waking that knocks us off our daily treadmill. Something inside of us stirs, leaving us raw and confused, questioning what we have come to know and believe.

What we do next defines our lives.

Do we gather the courage to begin to believe in ourselves and the signs of the magical interconnected world that surrounds us—in things beyond what we have been taught or have experienced? Do we risk undertaking a pilgrimage based on the signs and guidance that we have received, one that may lead to an initiation into our authentic power, purpose, and clarity? Into fully knowing, embracing, and embodying our reason for being here? Do we do whatever is necessary to move through the third season of waking and into the fourth season of living whole?

When we begin to transform ourselves, we will agitate and invite our closest relationships to transform as we reorganize the general status quo of our daily lives. As we begin to consciously move through the seasons of our lives, our choices may impact, threaten, or otherwise rattle the cages of those nearest to us. Everything that is familiar—both physically and emotionally—may be threatened. Our previous agreements with others may need to be addressed or revised, which may force those closest to us to face their own wakings, pilgrimages, and initiations.

Our other choice is to run away and fall back asleep, dismissing our direct experience of who we are, along with the interconnected magic of reality, as nonsense and unproductive. This is a choice that many people make, but this book is here to provide you with a different way of seeing things—a different and better story—that you can try out for yourself.

By becoming conscious of the seasons—eternal patterns that have shaped human experience from the very beginning of our species—we come to understand the deep meaning and purpose they have in our lives. By reflecting on, absorbing, and taking action in accordance with the secrets that the seasons hold, we can empower ourselves in extraordinary ways.

This book addresses the journey taken by every soul that lands on this earth in a human suit of skin and bones. The journey changes over time, moving through four distinct and typically nonlinear pathways that we will call the seasons, as follows:

- Season 1: **Being** (up to about eighteen months of age)
- Season 2: **Doing** (as we make our way in the world)
- Season 3: **Waking** (as we are initiated by the circumstances of our karma, DNA, and destiny) and
- Season 4: **Living whole** (whereupon we live and thrive at peak performance levels by fully embracing our spiritual awakening and our daily activities, goals, and interactions as one)

Lessons and Reflections

> ❝ Each day, each moment,
> I am growing INTO my power,
> into my dreams ...
> that is why I am here.

The best way to learn is our own genuine experience, so that's why this book is based on what I have gone through and the lessons I have learned throughout the seasons of my own lifetime so far. This includes my experiences with the visible and the invisible world, as well as what I have learned from my teachers, students, and colleagues.

My stories are then woven into the lessons, practices, and tools shared throughout this book. Sharing my experiences and stories helps keep my words authentic and real, and I believe in leaders who are real and unafraid of being authentic. As you will see, I'm very human and have experienced—and sometimes still experience—many common weaknesses and fears. As always, we have an opportunity to acknowledge and learn from both the fallibility and the magnificence of everyone we meet and to learn something valuable from every story we hear.

Throughout most of my journey, I did not possess something that would have come in truly handy: a decent, pragmatic map of the territory I was going through. Regret is the most useless emotion, so I do not "wish" I had known these secrets when I was growing up. As a teacher, however, I can't help but wonder how some knowledge of the broader wisdom context—of the power and benefit of understanding the simple but profound secrets of the seasons—would have impacted my life.

I feel so blessed to have had the courage to stay awake and work through my own seasons and to have come to the place where I am now, feeling honored, directed, and in some profoundly positive way obligated to share these secrets with you. There's not a day that goes by that I don't experience tremendous gratitude for all of this.

And from that place of gratitude, my hope for you is that if I provide a better and more accurate and useful account of what is actually going on, along with some interesting stories and lessons to reflect upon, you will have a deeper and more powerful perspective of the journey as you go forward in life. Just remember that every pilgrimage—every journey of initiation into waking up and living whole through the seasons of life—has powerful, life transforming, often disturbing, and sometimes frightening ups and downs, including mine.

Seven Years Later: Wake-Up Call

Let me tell you a story that begins ten years before this book came to completion:

> Spring 2010: *I was alone, walking in a nearby park, when the numbness returned to my limbs and the pain started filling my mind. Somehow, I managed to drive myself home. After my wife drove me to the hospital, I soon found myself lying flat on a hospital gurney in the ER of a modern American hospital, in fear, unable to control my body and incapable of speaking beyond a slurred babble. Hyperbright lights penetrated me from every angle, but I felt submerged in utter darkness—overwhelmed, helpless, and totally lost.*

Despite the situation I was in and the pain I felt while lying on that gurney in 2010, a distinct memory from five years earlier—from 2005—clearly played back through my mind:

> August 2005: *After experiencing several signs that I could not ignore, I had journeyed to Kathmandu to undertake a formal shamanic initiation. But just four days before the scheduled end of that month-long program, I found myself walking to the airline office through Kathmandu's dusty downtown scuttle, tail between my legs. I needed to change my ticket so I could leave early and return home immediately.*
>
> *In my business life, I am a driven achiever who never ever quits anything. But just a few days earlier, a small and mighty shaman had berated me over and over again, telling me I was truly not in my power.*
>
> *Before I could become who I was meant to be, he yelled, I had to uncover—had to come to terms with and honor—my own personal heritage. If I failed to do this, I would never fully embody my personal power or my reason for being here.*

In that moment, five years before finding myself on the hospital gurney, I knew without doubt that my next pilgrimage— my next personal pathway through the seasons—was to be found back home, in the United States. Part of me felt like I was running away, but I also knew with certainty that the remainder of my formal shamanic initiation would have to wait, and my next true initiation would come in a way that I could not plan for. Still, five years later, this was *not* what I was expecting:

> Spring 2010 (continued): *Full of bodily terror, the numbness that coursed through my veins rendered every muscle in my body useless. Time stretched out seemingly*

forever as things were happening to me that neither my own brain—nor top-notch experienced Western medical doctors—could begin to explain.

To the degree I had any faculties left as I lay completely numb and helpless on the gurney in 2010, an eerie feeling, like déjà vu but more intense and in real time, came over me. What I was feeling was curiously similar to the emotional agony that I experienced after my initiation in Nepal in 2005—*but* with a soul-crushing intensity.

The shamanic tales I had read and heard before prematurely departing Kathmandu five years earlier spoke of things in this world—entities, energies, spirits, patterns—that can dismember us, rip us apart, reduce us to our core, open us up, and force us to face our deepest soul wounds.

My cultural upbringing and supposedly sophisticated educated mind told me—even in the throes of agony on the gurney—that this was a completely irrational idea. But I could not ignore the fact that despite what my rational mind was saying, the feeling I was having was virtually identical to what I had experienced in Kathmandu, but more intense—and I'd never before or since had that feeling.

Spring 2010 (continued): *The words "You can't do it like this anymore" rang through my mind. In that moment, I knew that what I was going through was an initiation of shamanic proportions, and that I was being given a deep teaching that became the secrets of the seasons. And indeed, over the next year, the initiation that I went through was as horrific and excruciating as it was exhilarating and necessary.*

It took me a few years to come to understand what "You can't do it like this anymore" meant and to then process the vision and understanding I had been given into useful words and teachings. Today I know that "You can't do it like this anymore" is really the story of our species, and the secrets of the seasons are a way out of the bind we've gotten ourselves into—a guide to changing the dream.

My Job, Your Job

Through the story of my journey—as illuminated by what I have learned of shamanic teachings, the ancient wisdom of the elders, and my own experience—this book offers you the guidance to courageously stay awake and follow your own pilgrimage throughout the seasons into the purposeful life that is calling you.

My primary pragmatic goal throughout this book, then, is to help you recognize what season you are in and what that means for you, personally, right this moment. My conventional training and personal understanding of psychology, energy medicine, ancient wisdom, business, economics and investing, and physics will also play a role.

Let me be clear that while I am offering a set of concepts and way of seeing the world that can completely transform your life for the better, you're your own guru. (Or as is sometimes said, *guru* can be taken as short for "Gee, You 'R' You!"). There is a great paradox in finding and following a teacher and trusting while, at the same time, honoring your own inner wisdom and direct experience. That's really the entire point of this book: you are inherently a divine magical being with ever-ready access to all the guidance needed for you to perfectly unfold, evolve, and contribute your own special and unique gifts.

To facilitate this process, I am providing some background, telling some stories, and suggesting some tools and practices that were given to me to tickle that deep place in your soul that already knows. Most importantly, however, I am hoping to provide you with a sense of hope, excitement, gratitude, and resilience, so that regardless of your current life circumstances and current state of mind, you come to embody a sense of how and why you can transform your life from just surviving to positively thriving.

So, please, touch base deeply with your soul and place attention on it. If at first you have to use your imagination to think of yourself as a soul, then let me implore you to do just that: pretend, at least for a short time, that you aren't just a mind enmeshed in a pile of flesh that is here for an all-too-short period of time on a ball spinning over a thousand miles per hour through an unconscious universe. If you can do this—if you can expand your consciousness—you can gain a sense of resilience, perseverance, and hope that will help see you through any conceivable set of circumstances, regardless of what season you find yourself in.

As Lao Tzu said in the sixth century Taoist teachings *Tao Te Ching*, "A journey of a thousand miles begins with a single step."

After all, there is almost nothing more powerful than hope. You may not be able to see the magic down the road, but hope will let you feel that future magic right now and begin to amplify and direct it. And hope will let you see above and beyond the linear time frame we live in to see how your whole life fits together, why things have happened to you, and what your next best steps are.

During my initiation period in Kathmandu (which I will talk about later in the book), there were times when I felt completely lost in darkness, not knowing how to navigate "me" through this world I was living in. But still inside of me I always felt a flame that kept me alive and driven to live my purpose. If you find yourself lost in the darkness of the early phases of the third season, then focus on the flame, feed it with anything you have left inside of you, and make sure you don't believe everything you think. (Someone once said that just because you hear voices inside of your head doesn't mean they're your friends.)

You are here for a reason. You matter. There is a purpose to your life, and your soul and the universe conspire to support you in unfolding and achieving that purpose for the good of all. When you come to truly understand this—when you learn to place attention on the awareness that is your birthright and the gifts and signs that naturally and inevitably arise before you—you can embody an incredible power that rapidly expands, validates itself, and enables you to optimize every element of your life.

So go ahead. Suspend your disbelief. Pretend, just for a while, that you can experience the magic of your soul and the alive conscious universe working together to help you to be you. It only takes a microsecond to know—to remember or reawaken to—who you are, what you are supposed to be doing, and how you can move toward realizing your dreams and potential and making the world a better place.

> When you awake from the dream,
> you remember that everything in the dream is you.

You can do all that right now. Before you read any further, you can change the dream. Ask yourself what you want your future to look like as you tune into the feelings and images that come your way. Imagine a story in which you and those you love are thriving, happy, and vibrantly alive. What would it feel like to be living within such a story?

What would you see, touch, taste, hear, and smell? Who would you be spending time with, and what would you be doing on a daily and weekly basis? Give yourself permission to imagine one or more scenarios that would make you very happy. Just imagine it—feel it—and ask yourself whether you would move toward living in, through, and out of that story if such a situation were possible.

Embracing and Embodying a Different—Better—Story

" At all costs, please remember that you are here for a reason—that you, personally, matter—and that you play a critical role in the tapestry of the universe, even if, and perhaps especially if, your path is misunderstood by those around you.

This book presents you with a different alternative—a modern but eternally human story that embraces the timeless knowledge of wisdom keepers throughout the ages. You can believe in and make use of this story no matter where in your life—whatever season of your life—you may find yourself in.

By living through this alternative story or dream, by opening to and integrating the knowledge of who we are and why we are here, it becomes far easier for the inherently good and magical nature of each of us to fully unfold and then join in collective co-creation. That's why I am inviting you to try out this alternative perspective, to see whether it rings true for you and might make an extraordinary difference in your life.

This alternative story is full of many lessons for all of us— lessons that I, of course, first had to experience for myself. Then, after many years of coming into my own power and helping many hundreds of others do the same, I have focused the last several years of my life on consciously becoming a better teacher, someone capable of effectively sharing the messages and gifts that come through me so all of us can thrive: our species as a whole, our sweet Mother Earth and all of its inhabitants, and, of course, the sun, the stars, and the universe. The world is calling us in her many forms to awaken. Can you hear her?

Having been blessed to recognize, experience, and follow these teachings for myself, I have come to a point in my life where it is both my nature and purpose to now share the secrets of the seasons, very practical and testable wisdom that can help transform our species. But given that message—"You can't do it like this anymore"—it took me some time and help to process the magnitude and depth of what was being channeled through me into an understandable and teachable form. Ultimately, the seasons are our birthright, designed to help us express our being in full sync with our doing until our waking so we can live whole and thrive as individuals and as a world.

In a world filled with so much noise and so many gimmicky self-help formulas and weight loss programs, I implore you to open your heart, soul, and mind. This book took more than a dozen years to finish—something my wife tells me to not publicly admit—but ultimately my only plan for this book is to be impeccable, as I know this message can and will save and transforms lives. So if it does make a difference in your life, then please share it. Many of those you know may be ready to embrace the secrets of the seasons for themselves ... and the world is waiting.

Ultimately, I'm asking you to see if what I am saying feels true to you—if it resonates as valid, real, and useful, please open up a space within yourself for it to enter and land.

Can you hear me?

The Four Seasons

2

The Fourfold Seasons of Life
Upon arrival, I knew I was a pure soul.
First I thought I was *really something.*
Then I thought I was *really nothing.*
Until I knew I was *really everything.*

The first chapter introduced the concept of the seasons, the theme of this book. The journey taken on this earth, by every human, changes over time, moving through these four distinct and typically nonlinear pathways—the seasons—as follows:

- Season 1: **Being** (up to about eighteen months of age)

- Season 2: **Doing** (as we make our way in the world)

- Season 3: **Waking** (as we are initiated by the circumstances of our karma, DNA, and destiny) and

- Season 4: **Living whole** (whereupon we live and thrive at peak performance levels by fully embracing our spiritual awakening and our daily activities, goals, and interactions as one)

15

The next chapter will focus on the lore of teachings of the ancient shamans and wisdom holders—the indigenous leaders, healers, and medicine men and women found at the heart of tribal civilizations through history (and their modern descendants). According to many of these visionary leaders and healers, the goal of the soul throughout every stage of the seasons of life was clear: to come to understand and make use of a set of core lessons and tools to fully live life—what we'll call to *live whole*—and to give back as much as possible to the greater good.

But first, let us look at each of the four seasons in more depth. Familiarity and experience with the secrets of the seasons provide us with an understanding of the laws of our soul's nature. It also gives us some desperately needed context for thriving in a chaotic and often seemingly senseless world. An understanding of the secrets, of the twists and turns we must each go through as we move along the pathways of our lives, provides an extremely useful roadmap for waking and thriving during our precious time here on earth.

By becoming and remaining fully conscious—by truly being present *right now* in the season we happen to find ourselves in—we gain a deep understanding of who we are, how life works, and what we can personally do to make ourselves happier and more effective, as well as make the world a better place.

Knowing what season you or someone you care about is in—especially if you or that other person is in the throes of the third season challenge—can be a literal lifesaver in times of greatest darkness and despair. As we come to understand the secrets, we can grab the helm of our lives, align our doing with our being, and consciously co-create the dream we already find ourselves part of.

This is why the seasons exist in the first place: by understanding and attuning ourselves to them, we are able to consciously remember why we are here. This enables us to optimally learn, grow, awaken, and fully align our doing with our being so we can live whole. By entering into an awakened life—the life we have imagined and deserve—and living our dreams, we embody the ultimate essence of why we are here.

Let us now take a look at the seasons, one by one.

The First Season—*Being*

" Upon arrival, I knew I was a pure soul.

The first season, *being*, begins with being born. Here we are naturally and with no effort fully aware of who we are: a pure soul, a blessed incarnation of love itself. In the first season we experience ourselves as sacred, interconnected, and fully loved.

But the season of being is also a busy time. The soul at first does not really know where it is and must get used to the new body—the new skin suit—it has just landed in. Learning to cope with the reality of being awake and alive in the body we have just entered takes some effort. Similarly, entering into the collective dream the soul has also landed in at the family, societal, national, and global levels also takes some getting used to.

Being lasts roughly until the age of eighteen months and ends when the child looks at himself or herself in the mirror and recognizes that they are "in" a body:

> Prior to the age of eighteen months, infants do not seem to know that what they are seeing in a mirror is their own reflection. After eighteen months, they do. This can be shown by surreptitiously marking infants' faces with

rouge, so that they are unaware that the mark has been placed. When younger infants see their reflections, they point to the mirror and not to themselves. After the age of eighteen months or so, they touch the rouge on their own faces instead of just pointing to the mirror... (*Psychology Today*, 2012).

Starting around eighteen months of age, as we know we are in a body—as we know we are really *something*—the direct and immediate awareness of our experience of our soul's existence and purity fades over time. It is so much a part of us—like the air we breathe or the eyeglasses that we have on our face—that we take its existence for granted and forget it is even there. But no matter how deeply it may become buried, the knowledge of our true nature always remains alive within us. Ultimately, after all, it is who we truly are.

Our soul sings true to us throughout all of the seasons, calling us home. Having knowledge of our own nature comes in handy later on, especially during the worst of the transformational turmoil and challenging initiations eventually faced by all human beings. During these challenging times—especially in the second and third seasons—our deeply imprinted knowledge of the nature and purity of our own soul bubbles up to the surface. Like a goose or monarch butterfly knowing its time to fly south, it says "hi" to the rest of us, helping to initiate our process of remembering why we are here.

The Second Season—*Doing*

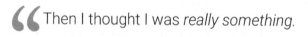 Then I thought I was *really something.*

The second season lasts from around eighteen months into early, middle, or late adulthood. Here, we mostly forget we are a pure soul and work hard at identifying ourselves as a thing—as really something—and try to make our lives work from that perspective. We try to fit in to the way things are—no matter how different we are, and no matter how crazy the world seems to us.

Then, as part of this domestication process, we fall asleep and produce the kind of thinking that identifies who we are as a thing. Put differently, our wild, pure, beloved, eternal essence is forgotten as we do what is necessary to force ourselves, as a thing, to fit in with all the other things that our conventional world consists of, insists on, and has collectively dreamed up into being. Some of this domestication is necessary and good, but while we are working on survival, we allow ourselves to become enculturated and fall deeply into the world's outer dream.

It's critical to recognize that this outer dream—which we experience as the real world—follows its own dream logic and holds so much power because it is collectively believed in by so many people across the world. That is, we literally dream the outer world into its current state. For example, you can see the outcome and power of the collective behavioral agreements people have with each other in the vast differences of automobile driving personalities seen in drivers from different countries, states, cities, or sometimes even just from a few miles away.

Think about it. Have you not noticed how differently people drive with different habits and styles around the world? And even in different states and regions within the United States? People from New York drive more aggressively than people from Maine, and people from the Midwest drive generally slower than people from California. It's like there is a secret unspoken rule of behavior—a collaborative dream.

In the season of doing, then, we practice aligning our doing with our being. As we attempt this alignment, we eventually remember and rediscover what does and what does not work, what does and does not feel good, and which paths overall to choose and which to forgo, like where to live and what to do for work. Later on, when we address the big picture of life, death, and the soul, we will see that each of us has some basic work we need to do in the second season, the season of doing, that comes from our karma and the early life experiences, conditioning, and domestication that in some way or another imprint each of us.

As we begin to awaken and come to see the nature of the outer dream and its logic, our situation becomes easier to understand, manage, and eventually transcend. Before then, we're merely sleepwalkers sleepwalking in a world that itself is but an outer dream, and often not a particularly suitable one. Still, it's important to note that forgetting is itself part of the process. When we forget and then remember, we are practicing aligning our doing with our being, which is the ultimate purpose of the second season.

The second season, the season of doing, is essential to our becoming who we are meant to be. It is our playground for practicing aligning our doing with our being, and the only way to get good at doing something like this is to practice. It's when we forget and give up—in part because we are not aware of the purpose of the second season—that the real trouble starts. In that case, we fall asleep, and we stay asleep.

The second season can also be particularly challenging for so-called old souls who see with acute clarity how the current collective dream makes absolutely no sense. The pain caused by the gap between (a) the reality these individuals see and experience and (b) the reality that on some level they know is possible is just too great to bear. That is, the split between what these individuals know from their first season and how they experience life in the second season is so great they develop issues that baffle modern medicine—and some even perish. Or these old souls may collapse from their inner semiconscious battle, give up, or fall asleep and temporarily buy into the collective dream, which is the best they can do given their level of spiritual understanding and of this dual reality.

Suppose part of someone is missing or traumatized—someone has lost part of their soul—like the child who was abused and as an adult has not yet worked through his or her soul wound. This person will, in the second season, unconsciously act out the imbalance of his or her soul malady, making it nearly impossible to fully align their doing with their being. The vibration of this person's soul becomes so impeded, thwarted, dysfunctional, and out of tune that it can no longer experience, remember, or sing its own true soul song.

Fortunately, that is exactly what brings us to the path for potential healing in the third season, the season of waking: initiations that wake us and provide the opportunity to move forward with our own desperately needed soul work and healing.

A Turn of the Wheel: Saved for a Reason in My Second Season

If you've ever been in a serious car accident or similar sudden crisis, you've experienced that moment when all of your senses become hyperacute and time seems to shift and slow down. Your body automatically moves into a hyperaware survival mode—you don't have to try to do any of this, your consciousness shifts time for you on your behalf until it's time to come back into your body. That's when you look up and ask, "Where am I? What just happened?"

I was a high school freshman in a tan denim jacket, and I was riding shotgun in my friend's mint condition antique '57 Chevy with four friends piled in the back. Our summers were filled with long days and nights of fun. Being in this huge car felt like hanging out in somebody's apartment.

It was midday, and we were off picking up supplies for our upcoming ski trip.

I leaned forward with my left hand to change the tunes—

—and the next thing I knew, I was on my back, on the pavement, with my left shoulder tucked in tight under the low side panel of the big green machine while the car was spinning. Everything slowed to a manageable tempo, as if my reality movie had been changed to slow motion.

The car was in a backspin. To this day I am not sure how, but somehow I was able to peer out beyond my feet in a slight crouch to see what was happening: Massive jagged tire treads were staring me down with a death charge. I knew that if I didn't keep holding onto the side panel to keep my head off the pavement that tore at my denim jacket and ground small pebbles into my skin, I'd be crushed right up the midline.

Then I looked to my right: A solid curb loomed near as the car continued to spin toward the side of the road. Even if I were able to hold on, if that curb kept coming, I would be split in two.

Then everything slowed down even more …

—reality changed, time shifted—

… and I saw/sensed/felt everything that was happening in a different light: Something had come to me and helped me hold on. Given my incredibly acute time-shifted awareness, I was sure that what kept me holding on was not just some freak adrenaline-powered biological survival reaction. Rather, a presence had come to me, stood with me, and kept me alive for a reason.

The car stopped. I looked around, saw the curb a few feet away, and observed that my passenger side front door was now mysteriously closed and latched. Instantly time accelerated to normal, as I heard the wail of approaching ambulances, police cars, and fire trucks.

Inside and outside the car, puddles of booze spread like blood. I hopped up, dusted myself off, and looked into the car to find my friends busily hiding what was left of the alcohol bottles we had just purchased for our upcoming trip. Even though the booze really was for the ski trip, I started panicking as I wondered how a bunch of underaged kids who had an accident driving around with lots of alcohol in their car would be treated.

I wandered around, and as my friends looked at me in disbelief, I was escorted to the ambulance and told to sit down and take off my jacket. They put some solution on my back and cleaned gravel out of my wounds. The police were sweeping up the broken glass as I stepped out of the ambulance into a new world. My friends gathered around me and led me over to one of the officers, who stood by the passenger door.

"Look here," he said. He pointed to an egg-sized divot on the inside of the door just below the passenger window. "This is some serious steel," he said. "I believe it is your point of impact. Hell if I know how the door opened and closed, and how you survived, but you are one lucky bastard. You sure you're okay? You really ought to accept a transport to the hospital."

The officer walked away shaking his head. When I got home, I told my parents nothing and shortly thereafter went on the planned ski trip.

By the time I got back to school several days later, it was clear I wasn't really the same person. For example, for a few weeks I experienced hall doors opening and closing in slow motion as I walked down the long corridors.

I felt a depth to me that I had not previously experienced but now knew had always been part of me. I was here—I was saved—for a reason. It was my responsibility to live my destiny. The mantra "saved for a reason" repeated continuously in my head, coming from a familiar but otherworldly source that I could not name or point to.

I truly was changed. I felt like a Martian shot out of a cannon into a two thousand–student high school. Everything around me was the same, but I was different, and things that previously consumed me no longer held my interest. It was as if the purpose of my life had somehow been revealed within me on some deep level, but I had no conscious idea what it was, and no choice but to let it unfold as I continued to move through the seasons of my life.

I had had a few similar experiences when I was even younger. When I was nine, I had a sudden knowing—a powerful inexplicable impulse—to move away from a light bulb seconds before it exploded, sending glass and metal shrapnel into the air. If I hadn't suddenly moved away in the nick of time, I would have definitely been injured and possibly even blinded.

And there was a grade school sledding incident that found me staring down a car tire that crushed the corner of my sled, just inches from my neck. As I crawled out from under the car, I ran into the woods in a state of semi-shock, hearing the echo of "You're here for a reason" reverberate through my soul.

I floated through my high school halls for the next few months. Awareness of the remarkable things that happened during and immediately after the accident would fade over time, but never leave me entirely. And often, in my reflective moments, I would find myself right back there in that moment—being supported to hold on, knowing that I was here for a reason. Like certain other special moments in my life, that hot spot would stay with me forever, beckoning me to reconsider the significance and ultimate meaning of my life. We'll discuss hot spots more in just a bit.

The Third Season—*Waking*

❝ Then I thought I was *really nothing.*

Over time—as we try so very hard to be really something while the forces of domestication are buffeting us about— experience helps teach us just how hopeless it is to try to come to grips with the ultimate reality of our souls in a world that has collectively fallen asleep and given rise to a sleepwalker-driven nightmare.

Realizing how hopeless it is to try to fit into such a world, at some point—for almost everyone—there is a period time (or multiple periods) during which arise feelings of despair, darkness, nihilism, and hopelessness. Teenagers naturally go through this season of initiation, but as sleepwalking adults we are generally ill-equipped to see it for what it is, and so the opportunity is missed.

A waking can originate from external life events and pressures or be inspired by internal events, feelings, and realizations. Sometimes it is subtle, coming to us as a coincidence or slightly odd feelings or memory about something that once happened. Other times, a waking can come directly and harshly—often in the form of a crisis in our personal or collective experience like a natural disaster or pandemic—which may lead us on a journey or pilgrimage of initiation. A waking provides an opening through the trees where the path was once dark, illuminating signs and guidance that have been there for us all along.

Finding ourselves lost in a dark wood, pathless and frightened, we experience what Western religion and archetypal psychology have called the dark night of the soul. Deep depression, relentless worry and anxiety, inextricable career and school pressures, and family, financial, and health problems, loss of a loved one—some or all of these feelings and circumstances come to dominate the experience of many (and possibly most) people.

Because many of us have little or no context for what is happening to us during this season, we tend to cling to the darkness and shame of our condition, rather than questioning it or looking for the deeper meaning.

But here's the good news: Experiencing such darkness is only the first stage of season three, the season of waking, which in many cases eventually leads to a breakthrough from darkness into light, from pain and distress into a real-time-lived sense that our lives are good and that the world is good. Season three, then, can bring us to an amazing place, but to get there we must first—each to our own needs and according to our own karma, genes, and destiny—experience one or more substantial initiations.

Such initiations, which come to all human beings over time, are the kinds of difficult and distressing life-quaking episodes that are designed to shake us out of our slumber. They enable us to become aware of the season we are in and invite us to face ourselves as we grow and evolve to new levels of understanding, capacity, and compassion. Often triggered by the actions of other individuals or external circumstances—whom we can think of as our teachers (or, in Carlos Castaneda's words, our "petty tyrants")—these initiations force us to slow down or stop entirely, and then change, grow, and evolve (or not).

As is abundantly clear, even if we make good decisions and the right hard choices—even if we become fully aware of the season we are in and what is going on and react as appropriately and effectively as possible—we are never in complete control of life's events and circumstances.

The only real option is to let the events of the current season fully unfold and take their natural course, because the trees ahead and bushes beside you are not lost (as David Wagoner said in a poem) and signs are all around you guiding you into your power. The best way to find ourselves is to become completely still, exactly where we are.

Placing attention on the season we are currently in can prove extraordinarily valuable. If we don't do this—if we don't give ourselves some context for what is happening to and through us—then the lessons being offered us by the current season will soon enough repeat themselves. Better to be fully present, become fully aware, and consciously move forward as soon as we are ready and able to.

The secret of the third season, then, is that initiations are ultimately incredibly valuable wake-up calls that open us to the potential for soul retrieval, soul healing, and fully aligning our doing with our being.

The Fourth Season—*Living Whole*

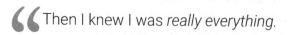 Then I knew I was *really everything.*

Finally, in the fourth season, after having broken out of the third season's darkness and into the light, we come to see, feel, and recognize our own true nature—that we are not just part of everything, but in some deep cosmic and very practical sense, we actually *are* everything. In this season, we have remembered—*re-cognized*—our true nature while also learning to function at ever-better levels of optimal performance and cooperation in the real world.

Similar to the concept of non-dual enlightenment, and also harkening to the Chinese concept of *Wu Wei* (literally, action without action), those in the fourth season find themselves effortlessly engaged in natural action. They do more of what needs to be done without struggle or excessive effort. The dancer becomes the dance; the athlete flies down the field in flow; and the religious practitioner experiences grace. And the consumer and investor become conscious, participating in the coming alignment of their actions and capital to help collectively rebuild our world.

Ultimately, in the fourth season of living whole, we must face a paradox: After all we have been through, what we do matters less than how we do it. Whatever we bring ourselves into fully is what matters most, and also somewhat paradoxically, we cannot bring ourselves fully into something—regardless of what it is—without already being beautifully aligned with it.

As we operate at this higher level, there is no strain from trying to grasp water—from chasing after something that can't be caught. Instead, day-to-day living becomes about playing with the flow that leads us home. Consciously doing this changes everything in our lives—we begin to dream a new dream. And, fortunately, there is a way of making it work easier and better, a kind of new operating system that allows us to thrive in the fourth season. The details of that soul system operating map and how to upgrade your own life with it will be discussed later in this book and in the leadership training programs I provide for individuals and corporations.

The soul system operating map is the spiral pathway we move through as human beings as life unfolds and the universe embraces itself and enacts its own self-knowledge. This is the big aha!

The secret, then, of the fourth season of living whole, is that once you are awake, there are no longer any secrets because magic is everywhere in a universe constantly conspiring to help us live a whole life full of purpose and fulfillment.

Here, then, actively remembering in a way that becomes real-time knowing, we find that everything—all of existence—is conspiring with a deep universal love on our behalf. Here, in the fourth season of living whole, we come to understand that lucky breaks and coincidences are actually signs, guidance, and support. And we also find our dreams coming to fruition more quickly than ever as we give them the love and attention they need to root in reality and transform our lives. We remember that signs are everywhere; we learn how to use them; and we find ourselves getting better at doing so as we experience, in real time, that this is what we are actually doing.

Experiencing the Season You're Already In

Spirit whispers to us in the gaps between our thoughts, in the space between the notes, in the pause between the breaths; take the courage to sit for a while and say ... hi!

After the eighteen months or so that we find ourselves living in the first season, the second, third, and fourth seasons can vary greatly in length, with some people staying in the second season for most if not all of their lives. Some old souls move along almost instantly into the fourth season early in life, but revert into the second or third seasons until an awakening comes.

The seasons, then, are not necessarily one way only or linear in nature. Someone lost in the dark woods of the third season can move back into the second season, pushing aside their dread and fear while redoubling their efforts to be really something. Similarly, someone can wake up and become permanently established in the kind of non-dual realization that constitutes the fourth season, but even in that season, a severe enough life shock, external global crisis, or trauma can pull them back into the second or third season, with another initiation or soul pilgrimage soon coming their way.

Fortunately, many people—more than you may think—come out the other side into the fourth season. These people know—or remember—who they really are and are able to put that knowledge into practice by living whole. They are, as the Bible puts it, "in this world but not of it." But as mere mortal humans, even these folks occasionally slip back into experiencing the dynamics of earlier seasons to experience more lessons.

Our stories—like our lives and our soul songs—are wonderfully unique, a reflection both of who we are to begin with and the wild vagaries of chance and destiny that have brought us to the present moment. What is not unique, however, is the great value brought to us by knowing what season we currently find ourselves in.

If you are aware of the season you're in, then you're much more likely to recognize a waking, magic, or an initiation as it occurs. With a knowledge of the secrets of the seasons, you can stay alert to the signs of the ever more purposeful life that is calling you. And that alertness can then spark whatever action is needed for you to follow the signs that lead you on a pilgrimage into claiming your power and fulfilling your destiny.

So make friends with the season you're in, and with the hours, minutes, and seconds that constitute it. Yes, I know the thought of making friends with a season that has you in the grips of depression or deep confusion or in a time of a global crisis is tough to hear, but give it your best. This means relaxing, slowing down, and being there fully with whatever arises, no matter how negative or intense it may seem (and then saying "hi" to it).

This simple but profound practice changes our lives the moment we enter into it and brings us to the extraordinary value of learning to slow down and lean into whatever it is we are experiencing. I am going to say it again because it is so important: The mere act of knowing that whatever you are going through has a deep purpose will in and of itself transform your situation over time.

We all go through different seasons throughout our lives. Depending on what season we're in, we may find that we don't fit in, things aren't working well, or we feel lost in an impenetrable darkness or even despair. But if you open to the cosmic wind at your back, if you become aware of the possibility and then the reality of the communications the universe is sending and the way it shapes events to reinforce those messages and assist us in moving forward—things can change for the better in a micro-moment.

So whatever season you find yourself in right now, even if you happen to be stuck in a season of doing without meaning or in a dark place—lost deep in the woods in a seemingly never-ending third season scenario where there may have been an initial waking but not much else has happened—please stick with me and stay the course, because the big picture—which you get to see later in the book—is likely much better than anything you can imagine right now. Remember: the universe is whispering to you and supporting you—in its own often mysterious but always magnificent manner—all the time. Always, without fail.

As soon as you become aware of this—as soon as you begin to slow down to more deeply experience what is going on and how your very own thinking about what is going on changes things—everything can shift. From procrastination into action, from overwrought thinking into clear feeling, from despair into focused action and dream management.

Even when we're surrounded by or lost in darkness, it's not like we have to take buckets and wheelbarrows of darkness away to feel better. All we have to do is light one candle to dispel the darkness. And once we become aware of the season we're in and the power of waking is activated within us—however conscious or unconscious we are of the process—good things start happening, which leads to a daily experience of optimal living and peak performance.

Ancient Wisdom Keepers as Modern Guides and Teachers

Shamanism is a path of knowledge, not of faith, and that knowledge cannot come from me or anyone else in this reality. To acquire that knowledge, including the knowledge of the reality of the spirits, it is necessary to step through the shaman's doorway and acquire empirical evidence.

—Michael Harner

So much wisdom has been around for ages, but let's begin by focusing on one of the most ancient of all, shamanism. Shamanism begins with the idea that the universe itself is alive and aware and that everything within it is interconnected on some level, just like it was at the Big Bang. And not only is the universe alive and aware, it is caring and compassionate. It is concerned for each part of itself—for you, for me—and lovingly communicates with each of us about who we are, what we should be doing, what our next steps can be, how we can best grow or take solace, and so on.

If this concept is a stretch for you, please hang in there—trust me, it will be worth it.

Further, the feedback we are given isn't random but is built around our soul's unique being and reason for being here. This feedback can take the form of feelings, intuitions, signs, visions, dreams, experiences with nature and power animals, and visitations while dreaming—or even while fully awake in our living dream—of family, friends, and lovers living or dead, and of all those who have passed before us, including our ancestors. We can also find our minds returning over and over to the memories I call *hot spots*, which are strangely vivid recollections of seemingly random times and places that nonetheless hold great charge for us.

Shamans and Ancient Wisdom Keepers

For tens of thousands of years, shamans and other ancient wisdom keepers have dedicated their lives to studying consciousness, the wisdom of nature, animals, and what they called spirit. Through many tools and techniques, including practicing the immense value of learning to slow things down and stay present regardless of what was happening, they learned how to connect to everything and access every level of their own inner being and act as a rainbow bridge to help themselves and their tribes and societies.

As you slow down and become fully present to and conscious of all aspects of your life, you give yourself the opportunity to see connections and patterns, to reevaluate how you have gone about doing things, and to pick new goals and methods of achieving them. Unfortunately, our so-called advanced society has dismissed this ancient wisdom heritage, just as it has dismissed the wisdom of elders generally. Our collective dream has become so full of itself we already think we know everything and are generally not open to learning anything new.

This dynamic is reminiscent of the story of the professor who, for many years, had heard rumors of a reclusive but enlightened sage known for his great wisdom. After much seeking, the professor finally found the sage in a far-off cave. The professor implored the sage to share his great wisdom.

The sage simply motioned, inviting the professor to sit down for a cup of tea. After attending his kettle, the sage brought out a cup and began pouring … and pouring … and pouring. The tea overflowed the cup, then out of the saucer, then onto the table, and then onto the professor's shoes and the floor.

"Stop!" shouted the professor. "Can't you see my cup is full?"

The sage responded, "You are very much like this tea cup, which is so full to the top, there is room for nothing else. When your cup is empty—when your mind is empty—then come back to me."

Similarly, like a water glass or the professor's teacup filled to the top, we have little or no room left in our minds to take in new information. All too often, we really think there is nothing of deep significance left to learn.

In the old days, while spirit itself chose who among a tribe might become a shaman, the tribal elders were charged with handing down specific traditional wisdom, tools, and practices. The wisest of these elders would pass down what they knew with little dogma, so that new and receptive younger shamans could apply what they learned to changing times.

In this process, some of the wisdom of the ancient shamans was lost, but much has remained alive and vital, passed down even to this day. When, for instance, a sacred tool is passed down from an elder shaman to a new shaman, it is quite appropriate for that tool to be used in a different way by the younger shaman. It is the essence of the tool that matters more than exactly how it has previously been used or is supposed to be used. This is the paradox of ritual.

Shamanism itself has never been coalesced into a single formal belief or organization, with a static idealized sales pitch or hagiography, which in part has enabled it to evolve over time.

Still, to make this guide to the secrets of the seasons as accessible and useful as possible, in this chapter I will cover the basic principles of modern shamanism and attempt to root those principles in a simple set of experiential principles and instructions. These principles are derived from the works of respected modern shamans as well as from other sources, teachers, and ancient wisdom keepers, including my own courageous students. They have taught me mightily as I have watched them transform their lives and, in so doing, have helped me refine my teaching.

[Note: The Bön religion, which predates the Buddhism that arrived in Tibet in the eighth century AD, can in some ways be considered a single but loosely organized religion. Similarly, shamanism has provided many indigenous tribes and communities with a sense of continuity, structure, and solidarity for hundreds—and in some cases perhaps thousands—of years.]

Some of what you'll find in this chapter and throughout the book will therefore be familiar to you—old news, even—for a couple of reasons. First, what works in the realm of pragmatic spirituality remains consistent over time and tends to be noticed—although not always diligently practiced—by aware teachers in all times and places. So if, deep inside, you already know a good deal about what works for you personally, some of what you find here may feel familiar or redundant.

Second, your soul already knows. Since I am intentionally aiming to speak to you directly on a soul level—soul to soul, as it were—you may be surprised to find that you personally have a kind of built-in access to a collective knowledge base that we can all tap into (whether that's based on Jung's collective unconscious, a collective human over-soul, the Akashic records, Big Mind, or a telepathic resonance built into the DNA of all human beings). Put differently, if I know it, then on some level, you may already know it, too, and that's one reason my words may sound, feel, or be experienced as familiar.

Given how much has been written on shamanism, spiritual growth, personal development, and similar fields, it is statistically impossible for me to put forth anything that has not already been said in one form or another by somebody else. Moreover, please remember that up to 90 percent of all communication happens beyond the words and language being used. Here, then, in this written form, I'm only able to communicate with you on a very narrow bandwidth.

Therefore, as you read, allow me to ask you to listen beyond your five senses—from the place of your own soul's great capacity to see, hear, and understand. If you are at a time or season in your life when you are ready to hear something new or important, the message in this book will ring out for you with a clarion call.

Principles and Practices

Shamanism and other ancient wisdom traditions have been around for tens of thousands of years or longer. These traditions provide answers, practices, and an overall context for living that may at first seem to fly in the face of rational discourse. And we all know what happens to ideas that go beyond the rules of the five senses and do not fit neatly into the conventional rational empirical mindset. Typically—especially in the modern era—such traditions are dismissed as irrational and primitive, and the great mysteries of life are at best given an hour at church or temple.

But as you already know, this is an intentionally psychoactive book, one whose perspective goes far beyond the brain and its five senses. Written from my vantage point, not only does this entire book originate from the consciousness of the shamanic, religious, and other ancient wisdom and scientific worldview, but it was designed to both *communicate* that worldview to you and to *activate* (or awaken) it within you.

One of the wonderful aspects about ancient wisdom tradition is that it demands direct experience and is skeptical of dogmas and absolute truths. This book is designed to awaken within you—really, remind you of—your own soul wisdom in every season of your life. This book itself, then, is merely a convenience—a finger pointing at the moon—meant to strike a resonant chord or light a spark that sets your own knowing on fire as you increasingly consciously travel through the seasons of your life.

The Alive Interconnected Universe

Let's start at the beginning: Everything in the universe is alive, interconnected, magical, and conscious (albeit in ways that may greatly differ from ordinary human consciousness). The entirety of nature—including human beings—is endowed with forces, energies, and spirits that interconnect all of physical and metaphysical reality, that bring the world to life, and that make everything from awareness to communication to evolution to existence itself possible.

A quick review of the language used by scholars of religion may be useful here. **Animism** is the view that everything in the natural world is alive, magical, and interconnected. This is close to **pantheism**, which holds that the divine and the physically perceivable universe are identical—or put differently, that everything is composed of an immanent god.

Even better for our purposes is the term **panentheism**—that is, the belief that god-like mysticism permeates and interpenetrates every part of the universe beyond time and space.

As such, seen in panentheistic terms, the shamanic worldview holds that there is indeed a spirit world beyond this one that is not perceivable by the five ordinary senses, but which nevertheless pervades, interpenetrates, and connects all living things, physical objects, and forms of energy. Similar notions can be found in the esoteric or mystical branches of Judaism (Qabalah), Christianity (Meister Eckhart and Hildegard of Bingen are good places to start), and Islam (Sufism). Arguably, Hindu metaphysics—which in turn gave rise to Buddhism—has long held a view quite similar to this.

It is an exciting time as the seers and scientists are coming together and where the scientific evidence of the brain-driven reasoning is catching up with ancient soul wisdom. If we pay attention, we will see that this is a time of potential great awakening for our species as we can now validate from the rational brain things that we have been told for ages through the mystics and seers and religions.

From a scientific perspective, the universe's expansion is accelerating. Physicists now understand that the universe is not what they thought it once was, there is more mass than previously predicted, way more in the form of dark energy.

This dark energy is the space between the spokes that make the wheel, the stuff of the universe that connects us all to everything beyond space and time. This is the stuff that saints, shamans, yogis, mystics, and religions have been pointing to for ages and, until now, was only known through direct experience or through faith in those who tell us.

Constant Caring Feedback

Another key principle is that the magical interconnected universe that we are all part of regularly communicates with us and is not indifferent to our situation or suffering. Instead, the universe orchestrates events, people, opportunities, and coincidences to maximize our growth, awareness, and awakening. Under this view, nothing is really happening *to* us, it is happening *for* us. We can best think of the events in our lives as hints—as signs—like a scavenger hunt leading us onto the path of our true power and destiny.

When I say this to you in these typed words, I am doing so from a place of experience based in my own journey and in the journeys of hundreds of others whom I've guided. I am excited for you to hear the message of this book from a place beyond your intellect. Following the logic of this second principle, my belief is you are reading these words for a reason, and it is my prayer that the words I am saying tickle your soul and move your body/mind into action.

Additionally, each of us is here for a reason—a specific purpose—and our soul's longing conspires with the universe to manifest our unique destiny. On the conscious level, you may not know who you are, and you may not know what your destiny, purpose, or true will is—yet. Or you may have felt you knew it once, but then you forgot it, lost track of it, or just gave up. Or you may feel that you know your purpose, but may not know how best to live it. Perhaps you felt that a distinct destiny, a potent purpose, and a unique reason for being here were meant for others, but not you.

Fortunately, you can always reconnect to your purpose and reason for being here. Your soul, in collaboration with the universe, is always gently—and sometimes powerfully—beckoning and invoking you to move toward your destiny. Like a wise, loving grandmother holding you on her lap and whispering wisps of wisdom in your ear, your soul continually sings its unique song to you. It invites you to harmonize and sing along as clearly and as powerfully as you can.

There is some spectacularly good news here: The living, loving interconnected universe sees to it that each of us experiences exactly what we need to experience to maximize our growth and personal evolution—to become who we truly are meant to be. The universe does this as gently as it can, but as firmly—and repeatedly—as necessary. If we don't get the lesson, whatever it might be, it will surely be repeated.

Even at this moment, as I make these final edits to this book, we are being called into a collective awakening through a global crisis in the form of a pandemic. Our mother is giving us a time-out to go to our corners and think about what we have done, and she is compelling us to wake up and to remember that we are all connected from the global markets and economies to the air we inhale and exhale.

[Note: Importantly, I'm not in any way saying that anyone asks for or deserves a global crisis or personal tragedy in life. Many things happen to us that are beyond reason, and we certainly don't ask for them or deserve them. And while I don't have answers for why these things happen, I do know that regardless of what happens, the events have meaning. So, just as I would never wish my own challenging early childhood experiences (we'll come to those later) on anyone or say they deserved it, I personally would not trade what happened or any of the experiences that made me who I am today. Without those experiences, I would not be me, I would not be here, and I would not be bringing you these words.]

Like the energy of unconditional love at the very heart of its nature, the universe constantly serenades us with signs, hints, hot spots, and assorted and sundry affirmations to prod us to wake up, evolve, and participate as the magical co-creative beings we always already were.

Being in the center of a loving universe that is giving us constant, caring feedback (and sometimes even the tough love of a caring parent) directly contradicts what most of us have been taught: that we receive no feedback because the universe is not alive and, in any case, we don't really matter in the first place. But this common view is as backward as the idea that the earth—not the sun—is at the center of our solar system.

A Revolution of Perception: The Heliotropic Soul

The idea that the sun—not the planet Earth—is at the center of our solar system goes back to at least the third century BCE. But it took Nicolaus Copernicus's *Commentariolus* in the early 1500s to ignite a scientific revolution that could not be turned back.

The Copernican revolution suggests a useful analogy. Just as the planets and all of the matter in our solar system revolve around an enormous central solar element, our lives are influenced by, respond to, and always ultimately turn toward our soul's deepest longings—that is, our lives revolve around a central soul core element.

Whether you know it or not, then, on some level you are always feeling, leaning into, and responding to the influence of your soul. In the Copernican revolution, it became clear that the immediately physically present planet Earth was not at the center of things. Similarly, in a personal Copernican revolution, you come to understand that what your own life truly revolves around is not your immediate experiences, emotions, and mental pictures—the output of your five-sensory dream—but the unique, potent, and eternal energy of your very own soul.

Hot Spots: Luminous Clues with Deep Meaning Imbued

 Hot spots are moments that stand out, illuminated in time and memory—sometimes, but not always, for obvious reasons. Like a trail of bread crumbs left by the universe working in cahoots with our heliotropic souls, hot spots help illuminate the path before us and point the way toward our destiny so that we can come into full alignment with our soul's greatest needs and our reason for being here.

I've already mentioned hot spots a couple of times. These are certain kinds of clues that come to all human beings over time: places, spaces, and traces imbued with luminous personal meaning and extraordinary significance. You can think of hot spots like partly submerged stones you can step on to get across a rapidly moving river. If you become very present, you simply know which stone to step on to get you across, each new stone embracing its role in being there for you so that you don't have to look back at the other bank to make sense of your crossing. When you are in step with the stones and their meaning, you are living whole in a state of optimal performance and natural grace.

Hot spots are not necessarily associated with dramatic crises or big life events such as marriage, death, or the birth of a child. They can and often do occur during these events, but, then again, they are often quite subtle, like the sweet smell of your grandfather's pipe smoke. Suddenly the sensation pops into your head—years or decades later—and you wonder why that smell stuck with you, what it meant, and what it was leading you to.

Quite frequently, if you try to explain a hot spot to someone else, they just won't be able to get it. But it doesn't matter that other people may not understand because hot spots are of a deeply personal nature and to some extent always stay with you, like a recurring dream. They have the vivid quality of a déjà vu experience; as you experience them, there's no doubt that something is really going on.

Memories of hot spots enter into the gaps—the quiet times of daydreaming while waiting for a phone call or meeting to start, or a commercial to pass, or that short sweet moment before falling asleep. In an instant out of time, you suddenly find yourself back in that spot—in that time, place, and memory—and a feeling in your body is activated as if the hot spot were now, like when an old song plays and instantly you find yourself thinking back to holding hands with your first crush.

It is said that Einstein used to sit with a glass of water in his hand. As he was about to fall asleep, he would be jarred awake by the thought of spilling the water. It is in moments like these—in the gaps between waking and liminal consciousness—that magic and hot spots can best be found, hiding beneath the structures of ordinary consciousness.

Hot spots are like bread crumbs that have been dropped throughout your life that are designed to lead you back to your true self, your soul … when you are ready. They are treasures that may stay a mystery for most or even all of our lives, in part because we have not been taught that they exist or matter. But if you give your own hot spots the attention they deserve, something incredible happens. The simple act of intending to honor your hot spots—and the feelings and memories associated with them—begins to activate and illuminate a trail of bread crumbs that will guide you back to remembering who you really are and why you are here.

Cultivating, Remembering, and Warming Up to Your Hot Spots

Regardless of how lost or cynical we may become, we are always being guided. And if we take the courage to remember, to listen carefully, and to drift into a daydreaming kind of energy as we scan our past, a number of hot spots inevitably stand out.

So take some time to think back to remember and to experience those lucid moments beyond reason that stand out in your mind. They may originate in your childhood or school years, or they may be from just last week. Feel into them. Feel into their meaning and the direction they point you in.

Remember: your own personal hot spots may hold no overt meaning, and they don't have to be part of something as dramatic as being tossed from a car, like one of my memories. Yet there will be something about them that repeatedly holds your attention and curiosity in a special way. They may even come to you when you are sleeping in the form of a lucid dream. You likely will have no idea why you often journey back to a particular smell, sound, or scene in your mind, but as an important clue, hot spots have a way of holding your attention and re-revealing themselves at the most opportune moments.

If a particular hot spot or set of related memories comes up in a regular fashion, try to welcome it in and get close to it, say "hi." There is meaning in there somewhere, a veiled beacon softly but persistently drawing your attention to something of importance. You can think of it like planting a flag on that hot spot—not to grasp to know its meaning in that instant, but to mark it and hold the awareness in the back of your mind so when more clues appear you will be able to put the pieces together. Living this way makes life fun, like playing one big scavenger hunt leading to meaning and purpose!

Slowing Down to Orient, Stopping to Transform, Cooperating to Thrive

> I dreamed I was a butterfly, when I awoke I wondered ... was I a man dreaming I was a butterfly, or a butterfly dreaming I was a man?
>
> —Lao Tzu

If a part of you was hoping that at some point in this book I was going to reveal a secret esoteric practice—like putting your thumb in the air, twisting it three times, and then having a drink of slightly salty water while standing on your head—

then you will be disappointed. But there is a fundamental basic practice or modus operandi worth adopting, one embodied and embraced by nearly all of the world's spiritual and religious traditions, one that can transform both your life and the world: When things are tough, there is nothing more important than slowing down and staying present—regardless of whatever it is exactly that is going on or going down—and then stopping and having the courage to be present with it and say "hi."

The value of slowing down and becoming present was demonstrated to me by my tai chi master when I was in my twenties. As a gentle strike was directed toward my body, I nervously fumbled and anxiously maneuvered my way out of the blow and found myself proud, off center, and with my weight on the edge of my heels.

"Invest in loss," he said. "When you rush through the experience, you may entertain your ego with a temporary win, but in doing so you have robbed yourself of the lesson. Instead, settle into the moment and allow yourself to lose." You may feel temporarily "de-feeted," but you will have gained a deeper understanding of the lesson; "glue yourself to the moment and shift time." This form of action is counterintuitive and takes training to adopt because we are evolutionarily hardwired to react in fear and avoid pain and loss. In the stillness lies the greatest power.

You may not like the discomfort (whatever it is); the situation may make you feel emotionally or physically awful; and you may not know how long the lesson is going to last. But if you stay present with it—if you touch the teaching with your soul and see your circumstances within the greater context of your divine being—you will know that within you is not just greatness, but an eternal core essence that is so valuable the entire universe conspires to assist it.

But also remember self-compassion and always give yourself the gift of an eject button. If feelings get too big—if emotions become too intense while you are gluing yourself in the moment, then go ahead and consciously bail out—eject yourself from the moment.

Whatever detail of your personal pilgrimage originally persuaded you to pick up this book is no longer important because you're here now. There's nothing more I could wish or want for you and our world: to be completely, really, fully here—right now—just for a second, or as long as you can maintain. So let me ask you to try something: Take in a deep breath, slow down, and then maybe even … stop! … just for a short while. Just "be" for a moment or two and watch your breath as it rises and falls.

By choosing to slow down, working with your breath, and placing your attention in the moment, you have changed things—maybe by only a little, but maybe by a lot. (Later on I'll focus on a practice that shamans and other wisdom keepers call *stalking*. Very different from meditation or mindfulness, stalking is a powerful tool that when diligently applied can transform your life.)

You may have heard of the butterfly effect, which can be defined as the phenomenon that occurs when one small change in a complex system brings about larger changes elsewhere. So if a butterfly fluttering its wings in Rio de Janeiro can change the weather in Chicago, what effect might come from your slowing down and placing awareness directly on you, yourself, and your relationship to the big picture?

That butterfly, you may also know, was itself once an entirely different creature—a caterpillar. Like all caterpillars, once hatched and in its larval state, it spent most of its time seeking and eating food, starting with the leaf it was born on.

Eventually, when the caterpillar was done growing, it entered the pupa stage and literally cocooned itself into a third season as it turned into a chrysalis. At this point the activity of what was the old larval caterpillar slows down and stops completely.

> What the caterpillar calls the end of the world, the Master calls a butterfly.
> —Richard Bach, *Illusions*

Then something truly amazing happens. Within the cocoon, a small number of imaginal cells, sticking to their own genetically encoded time line (their own dream), seemingly appear out of nowhere. These cells turn into imaginal discs that become the major external structures of the glorious creature known as the butterfly. These imaginal cells, having become part of imaginal discs, start growing, multiplying, and working with each other to ensure the eventual complete transformation into a butterfly.

Importantly, if these imaginal cells did not fully cooperate and collaborate with each other, none of them would survive the attack of the pupa's immune system, and the butterfly would never finish its metamorphosis. These imaginal cells are your soul's DNA, longing to be activated amid an internal and external world filled with sleepwalking antibodies.

What if slowing down enough to access your own pure imagination—an inherent property of the pure soul that you always were and always will be—is enough to initiate a metamorphosis of your own? And what if cooperating with others was essential for that metamorphosis to come to full fruition? And what if coming together internally as well as collaborating with this butterfly dream of a better world was enough to withstand the old immune system that is fighting us?

Living a Longer and Happier Life?

There are two other huge advantages to learning how to wake up, slow down, and immerse yourself in the present moment, especially if you are having a positive or pleasant experience.

First, by slowing down, your experience of the moment—and time itself—literally stretches out before you. The more you slow down, the greater and richer your subjective experience will be. And the greater and richer your subjective experience is, the longer you take to experience and appreciate whatever is going on, and the longer you will effectively live. It's really just that simple.

Second, by taking in the positive or pleasant experiences, you literally rewire your brain to have even more positive experiences. "Neurons that fire together, wire together," as they say.

Pause for a moment and try this simple exercise my nine-year-old daughter taught me:

1. Breathe in from your nose and smell the flower.

2. Breathe out your mouth and blow out the candle.

3. Repeat three times.

Stalking: The Power of Active Self-Reflection

Learning how to slow down and be present is a fundamental requirement of the practice known as stalking. Stalking is watching, seeing, and reflecting on our own minds, feelings, and being—particularly our brain's thoughts. We watch ourselves with acuity, seeing where our thoughts are.

Practicing stalking begins with slowing down to the present moment, whether that is conceived of as mindfulness, meditation, or conscious breathing. Imagine, again, that your thoughts are like wild animals: If you wanted to get close to them, you would be as quiet as you could.

There are many ways to practice stalking, and when you become proficient at stalking, you can practice it nearly all the time. You can easily expand your stalking practice beyond just your thoughts to include your feelings, sensations, and any messages that are coming to you from the outside world or from your own inner realms. The more you stalk yourself, the better you'll get at it, even as it takes less effort over time to remain fully aware of everything you are thinking, feeling, and experiencing.

How do you practice stalking? Just watch what's happening. You are not trying to quiet the mind. If you find yourself psychoanalyzing your thoughts, feelings, sensations, or any inner or outer messages that you become aware of, just watch yourself do that. Stalking is just about watching. When your mind wants to do more than watch, just watch your mind doing that.

Stalking sounds so easy but in practice can be quite difficult. Why? Your brain experiences itself as having two main functions: creating problems and solving them. (Of course, your brain also keeps all of your internal systems functioning, such as the autonomic nervous system that automatically regulates bodily functions like heart rate, digestion, breathing, and so on.) When you strip your brain of this dual focus, you confuse it and make it angry. Then, in response, your brain will find ways to create new problems so that it can do its job again.

The other reason it can be difficult to master stalking is because we have fallen into the delusion that we *are* our brains—so pulling ourselves out of something that we have come to believe we are is a challenging puzzle for the mind and creates an intense resistance from the mind. As a result, it takes time and effort to grow ourselves out of that mistaken model.

How to Stalk

1. Find a quiet place to sit where you won't be disturbed or disrupted.

2. Close your eyes and relax your breath and body.

3. Play the stalking game:

    a. Get ready to watch your thoughts by labeling them as future, past, present, or not sure. For example: As I am writing this, I just paused to stalk, and my mind immediately went to thinking about the lunch I was eating a few hours ago. That, of course, was a past thought, so I would internally label it as such.

    b. Once you catch a thought and label it, do this next step: Take a deep breath in as you hold onto the thought and, as you exhale, label the thought with the appropriate label (past, present, future, not sure) and let it go.

    c. Come back to watching your mind and begin again.

In my experience from teaching stalking to hundreds of people, I know your brain will quickly attempt to convince you that this simple practice is a waste of time. Ignore your brain and stick with the practice. It will transform your life if you allow it to.

When you are stalking yourself, you may come up against a recurring thought, like being stuck in a maze with a big fat rat. If this happens, please consider two courses of action:

First, give yourself the permission to use the eject button. The eject button is like a self-compassion cord that you can pull if the emotions attached to a thought bring along a wave of feelings that are too big to handle. It is okay if this happens—you are onto something important, but don't rush it.

The suppressed wounds that so many of us have neatly tucked away will be brought to the surface by stalking at just the right time. Trust that the day will come when it will be time to devour the big fat rat that has been scurrying around in the darkness of your subconscious. Anything that you have not looked at for a long time, and that has been manipulating you in the dark of your subconscious, will likely appear as a monster when you first see it—so be kind to yourself and don't rush the process.

Second, know that you are illuminating something that already exists so consider using the following imagery while you are stalking yourself:

You are a bird in a tree or on a wire looking down. Below you see many mice scurrying around on the ground. These mice are your thoughts. Your job is to simply observe the mice. But eventually you may see a big fat rat appear—a thought that grips you in some deep way.

But if that fat rat continues to show up time and time again during your stalking sessions, it may be a sign that it's time to fly down and devour the rat. This is best done with the help of a friend, shaman, or trained therapist. By devouring the rat, you will move beyond limiting subconscious stories that have held you back for years or even lifetimes.

Doing this will release a tremendous amount of wasted energy (soul entropy) that comes from holding onto this soul wound story and directly addresses your loss of energy, chi, or life force. In addition, you will avoid the subconscious unintended result that often comes from holding these wounds out of our conscious sight—namely, the acting out of these soul wounds sometimes referred to as our shadows to others or ourselves. For example, the abused child who becomes an abuser to others or themselves.

But remember, stalking is for stalking. While there will be a time to devour rats, that is something different.

Give It a Go

Go ahead, then, and slow down, and with regard to the next thought you have, label it either as past, present, or future. Once you have labeled it—once you have caught that thought—breathe it in with a deep breath and then consciously let it go. It's as if you are in a field catching butterflies, and once you catch one, you take a big breath in and then let the butterfly and your breath go at the same time.

And then catch another thought, label it, and breathe it in and out and let it go.

And then try stalking with any feelings, sensations, or inner or outer messages that may be coming your way.

Alternatively, once you've stopped and slowed down—once you've seen yourself seeing the obstacle and not overreacting to it—it may then become perfectly apparent to you that action is needed—for example, that you need to devour that big fat rat or shine the full light of your heart on the darkness you've encountered. And the work that we do with each other—in families, in consciousness businesses, in workshops dedicated to living whole—can also be invaluable in helping each of us move through and beyond whatever has held us back.

Soul Fragmentation and Retrieval

Part of your soul can actually fragment and leave you when you are experiencing chaos, pain, fear, or severe unhappiness or despair. Parts of us—and sometimes large parts—must become unconscious and even split off to emotionally survive a trauma. (This is much like the conventional psychological theory of overwhelming shock, pain, or distress leading to a fragmenting of the self in cases of true multiple personality.) Similarly, from the spiritual shamanic perspective, when a trauma is too great or there is too much pain, a piece of our soul can be literally split off, sundered, and left behind at the moment of crisis.

For example, when I encounter someone who has been through significant abuse in their life, there is always *the* moment, *the* place in this lifetime, where that piece of their soul was split off and still actually resides.

Just like an overwhelmed body can go into shock and shut itself down by going into survival-and-protection mode, the soul too has its limits. If sufficiently overwhelmed, the soul fragments. If the event that caused the overwhelm is too intense, that piece of the soul may be left behind and not reunited until the person is ready to directly and consciously face the moment and the place where the trauma originated.

For example, you will learn later on that the breakthrough that delivered me from the trials of the third season and into the fourth season's living whole very much required that I return to a specific moment to encounter the splitting off that had happened to me at a very young age.

Traditionally, what a shaman will do—at the appropriate and impeccable moment—is to journey to that time and place and bring back or retrieve that soul part for the client so they can live whole. (Similarly, there are times when a shaman must remove something that is stuck in or attached to someone that does not belong and that is harmful.)

If someone is working with a psychologist or psychiatrist, talk therapy or regression work amounts to a similar process. The Western mind doctor goes back with the patient to the time and place where whatever it was actually happened, and from there, it is possible—at the right time and with the right support—for the patient to relax, allow, let go, and initiate healing.

What's particularly useful and elegant about the shamanic perspective is that it's not encumbered with goals or labels. Very simply, part of your soul has left, or was torn out or nicked, and to be a fully empowered and capable human being—in order to be fully healed and live whole—that part of you needs to be retrieved.

Unfortunately, not only are there many fragmented people desperately in need of a soul retrieval or other healing, but the overall way we live together on this planet is also desperately fragmented. As a species, instead of operating in harmony with others and the natural world and living healthfully and happily on this planet, we operate through competition and scarcity:

"There's not enough, and there's never going to be enough, so I better push ahead as hard as I can to get mine now!"

So while capitalism has lifted many from poverty and provided many technological wonders, it is also now killing us, in large part because capitalism as it now exists has lost a piece of *its* soul. In the name of making a profit, the needs of human beings, animals, and the natural world have been placed last, and ways of living healthfully and wholly—living whole— have for the most part been lost, forgotten, or buried. We are incredibly fragile. Nearly half of the people in the US have less than $400 in their bank account, so they are one missing paycheck or illness away from a financial crisis.

What we need is a new operating system—new rules of the game—to compensate for the way the human condition leads us to unconsciously and seemingly automatically abuse the rules of capitalism.

Unfortunately, we are unconscious of the whole systems perspective that takes everyone and everything into account (including animals and the natural world) when measuring success, including the costs and impacts of externalities. Despite how far our bodies (including our brains) have in some ways evolved, in many other (often determinative) ways, we still operate as primates ruled by fear and greed.

As a result, we often use the modern tools (that were once pointy rocks and sticks) of money or capitalism as a weapon of control and abuse rather than as a means to uplift each other and repair the world. Money and the markets are now a significant part of the dream that we have created, and including the discussion about capital and our consciousness is a vital component of our way home to wholeness.

This topic will be addressed in detail in my upcoming book on the nexus of consciousness and capital and can be found in the work I do at Conscious Capital Wealth Management and in my work in support of the United Nations called the Future of Capital—both can be found on my website (www.LawrenceFord.org).

We need to globally overhaul the game we are playing, and these rules of the game are built on the core operating system and belief of economics. The tools that we are so familiar with (money and capital markets) are merely modern day sticks and stones. From the very beginning, we need to recognize and deal with the reality that as human beings, power really can corrupt, and as British politician Lord Acton said, absolute power really does corrupt absolutely.

Many studies—such as Philip Zimbardo's famous Stanford prison experiment in 1971 where the students playing guards ultimately began torturing those playing inmates—as well as our experience with expensive cars running stoplights (the more expensive the car, the more likely the driver will push past safe limits) support the notion that power and compassion are inversely related.

As a species, we're just not very good at managing power and looking out beyond our own narrow, immediate desires. Neuroscience has taught us that as our power increases, our capacity for empathy decreases. This feature served us well as we stepped out of the cave to slay the saber-toothed tiger, but this hidden, unevolved human feature that lies below the surface of our awareness is contributing to the destruction of our species. As we wake up to this possibility, the single most important action we can each do is to know our ultimate weakness and be conscious of it.

Moreover, with the general loss of nature and the wild, the huge population explosion of the last 125 years, and the movement of most of these people to urban areas, capitalism has put a certain twist on things that has taken most of us to task. It's absolutely critical, then, to retrieve whatever might be lost from you personally and reintegrate it—whatever has been fragmented and must be gathered up and healed—so that you can also join in with others in bringing sensible solutions to the world.

The dream we are living is chock-full of desires and addictions for endless consumption, growth, and acquisition. We have fallen into this dream believing that our planet is an endless warehouse filled with resources and that growth at any cost is always good. To counter this dream, we need to wake up and remember that we are all one and that our purpose in life has always included giving back.

Aligning *Doing* with *Being* in the Second Season

4

Each day,
each moment,
I am growing
—INTO my power,
my dreams
... that is why I am here.

In the first season of life, up to eighteen months, we aren't really thinking or questioning. We just know we are a beloved soul. In the second season, everything changes. We begin dancing with our soul—mostly unconsciously—in an attempt to align our doing with our being.

The universe, of course, is always being supportive, with all sorts of signs, synchronicities, and bits and pieces of magical interventions coming to our aid, sprinkled in with some beautiful hot spots that we can track back to later, once we become more conscious and are on the road to our big lessons and initiations. But most people miss all of this, and that makes perfect sense because the world we find ourselves in is not particularly conducive to our true nature or to discovering that we can have a profoundly positive impact on the waking dream we collectively co-create and find ourselves within.

Instead, we find ourselves fighting to fit in, struggling to learn our place and find our pathway. We take our ego and separateness very seriously and begin working our way through the social context we find ourselves in. We go to school, grow up, meet somebody, and maybe marry or partner with them. We have a family, we develop a career, we make a nest. It's all part of the general consensus social goal of developing and becoming a real grown-up, a separate person who can make their way in the world and function independently.

During this process, nearly everyone—certainly including me—falls asleep and loses sight of the big picture. We often stop experiencing the magic and stop seeing the signs, the hot spots, and the lessons that are coming our way. We curse our terrible luck—whether in health, relationship, career, or global pandemics—instead of seeing the initiation that may be beckoning.

A World of Addicts

A related problem is the addictions that people fall into, addictions that can destroy or even end lives. Let's look at addictions from a new perspective.

Addictions can be thought of as a panacea for avoiding the pain of not experiencing and achieving our actual purpose and reason for being here. Our addictions guarantee us that we will be pulled out of the moment. And because we are always yearning for something in the future while we are in our addictions—something more and better—our addictions themselves constantly draw us out of the moment and pull us away from experiencing or having to deal with our inner discord. With our soul songs out of tune, and our being and doing misaligned, addictions are a creative, albeit subconscious, way to temporarily address our inner discord.

Think of it this way. When we are not being ourselves or living in our truth and power, and an inner imbalance is always stirring around inside of us, it's like walking around with a small pebble in our shoe or listening to the background hum of an air conditioner. For a while we can put these annoyances out of our mind and conscious thoughts, but sooner or later the discomfort becomes too big to ignore.

And because this is all still unconscious behavior, we unconsciously turn to self-medication to help drum out the pain of our internal discord. Addictions are the drug of choice since they act as the perfect short-term remedy to temporarily extend the deep feeling of sadness and pain our soul feels from being out of alignment with our life.

Addictions, in fact, provide a double short-term benefit. First, they provide an immediate distraction to take us away from the present moment of feeling the discomfort that could otherwise no longer be ignored through the usual means, like just ignoring the pebble for a while. The second added benefit of addictions is that even when we are not in the middle of the addictive act, whatever that might be, part of us is still longing and yearning for—and subconsciously planning for—the next fix to pull us out of the moment and again temporarily helping us avoid facing the pain.

Such addictive behaviors then begin to create new chemical pathways that trigger physical longings, and the resulting vicious cycle can spin us into a free-falling trap of a third season that we feel we can never escape. (Like with everything else in this world, other factors are involved here, like the biochemically addictive qualities of a certain drug that can immediately alter the chemical imbalances of the body and take you down a dark path with a single use.)

To address the epidemic-sized problem of addiction, we must deal with the core issue that drives it: a disconnection from our doing and our being. And instead of classifying some addictions as more acceptable than others in the eyes of the society, and judging those with certain addictions with such extreme prejudice, we can greet the addictive person with love, acceptance, and inspiration.

With the right perspective and understanding—knowing that they are somewhere in the second or third season, simply lost in a dark wood—we can offer a loving hand and help pull them up and out of it so they can see themselves and begin to wake up.

While some addictions are more socially acceptable than others—for example, Americans on average check their smartphones 80 to 300 times a day—addictions are essentially all the same and serve the same function, which is to keep us distracted from our pain. As those experiencing discord in the second season become aware of that discord on a subconscious level, they self-medicate against the sadness they feel from being so misaligned. Our society tends to see addicts as weak and broken, but, instead, they can be seen as just being one season from awakening and two seasons away from living whole.

Driven to Distraction (Think of It This Way)

A useful metaphor for understanding the second season of life—when we really think we are something, requiring domestication to fit in with all the other "things"—is the automobile.

Remember when you first started driving a car? Everything was unfamiliar. Everything had to be carefully thought through. The blinkers did this, the right foot pedal made it go faster, and the big left one stopped all motion—very important to know where the pedals are and how to use them.

Well, this is roughly what it's like when our soul begins to become domesticated in its new body as we grow up and move through our educational, career, and family life pathways. We have to learn how to operate our body and do all sorts of tasks with it to fit in.

But eventually we find ourselves attached to the car, even though we're actually a soul driving the car. We lose touch with the fact that we're a soul that has created its identity around a car (or a body) and think we actually *are* the car (or the body), and this is how we forget who we are and fall fast asleep in the outer dream.

The good news: no matter how bad your situation, as soon as you wake to the reality that you were only identified with the car (or body) and never actually were it, hope arises, and a light appears that helps usher you into and through the third season.

Of course, many good, wonderful, exciting, blissful, heartfelt, and rewarding experiences happen during the second season as well—friends, family, and everyday teachers share their beneficial wisdom as to how to navigate this world. We are supposed to have fun and enjoy this life; it is our birthright. One of my favorite sayings at work and in life is this—when in doubt, play.

Ultimately, we're all here to learn lessons and enjoy our voyages around the sun, and our lessons become part of our strengths, and those strengths are channeled into our reason for being here and amplify our ability to give back. Essentially, the practice of aligning our doing with our being is the dance that we all participate in—falling asleep, waking up, remembering and digesting our hot spots, having initiations, going on pilgrimages—all of which are designed to make us stronger and give us the ability to truly be in our power.

Going to and through life school—practicing aligning our doing with our being—is a big part of why we're all here. Some of what we experience along the way is truly terrible. We wonder why it is happening, and often, it's so terrible we can't possibly imagine that there is a higher purpose involved. But there is always a higher purpose involved, although it may take years to see what it is or have the cards of destiny unfold in such a way that everything makes sense. For example, as you will soon see, an unexpected—and for many, controversial— sign came to and through me early in life, one that took me years to understand and come to grips with.

Channeling a Sign of My Future, a Symbol of the Past

I can remember the feeling like it was yesterday. Sitting at my fifth-grade school desk—the old kind, with connected chairs—I was taken over by a powerful impulse to doodle on the piece of paper in front of me. I'd never seen it before, but somehow the symbol I'd drawn felt familiar. Drawing it felt good—not like making a great basketball shot or getting other kids to laugh—but deeper somehow, and seeing this symbol on my white paper inside my three-ring binder brought me a sense of peace.

Without thought, my hand followed precise and clear inner directions: Start on the upper righthand side, go straight down, then to the left, then straight down, with each segment the exact same length. Then start at the top left and repeat the process in reverse so the lines intersect. Then finally, as if to put a bow on it, the image is wrapped with a circle around it.

In the zone, ignoring the sound of the teacher's chalk squeaking on the blackboard, I was consumed with mastering the drawing. I knew in an instant that I had received a sign, a lucky charm to guide me through life—perhaps the most important symbol I would ever know. At the same time, it was not something for me to search out or chase down the meaning of—this paradox of yearning but not taking action is now comfortingly familiar to me, but for an eleven-year-old this notion was impossible to process.

In the days, weeks, and months that followed, I would regularly find myself spontaneously drawing the symbol again and again. While the design was simple, I was compelled to draw it just right—impeccably correct.

I felt the symbol calling to something deep within me. Despite how compellingly significant I felt the sign to be, something wiser than I led me to know that everything would be revealed in good time. Later, following a dramatic reveal halfway around the world (which I'll return to), I would learn what it was: an ancient Buddhist symbol at the heart of the Bön tradition that I was to be initiated into.

To this day, I spontaneously notice versions of the symbol wherever I go and have collected some nice examples that I keep near at work, home, and play—despite the sometimes controversial interpretations of the symbol's meaning.

Based on my experience, I have some advice for those to whom symbols come unbidden. Even if they seem to make no sense—and worse, even if they seem to be a symbol that has represented the essence of evil and thereby violate every ounce of your nature—you still need to trust what comes through you. In my case, I could have dismissed this symbol, this sign of my future, and bought into the prevailing perception that what came through me represented evil.

I did not dismiss it, and, in retrospect, I can see the beauty of this lesson for myself and for those reading this. Even late in the writing of this book, I found myself contemplating about even mentioning this symbol and how it came through me because I feared that because of the understandably overwhelming negative emotions it evokes (because it looks somewhat like the swastika that was turned at a forty-five-degree angle and used for the most evil crimes beyond imagination), it would distract from the messages and meaning of this book.

Instead, I see now that the bigger lesson here is that we each have to trust the signs and symbols that come to us despite whatever our rational minds might say or how society might judge us or how one evil person in recent history has given a different meaning to a symbol that had represented such good for hundreds of years prior. This is *your* journey, *you* are here for a reason, and the signs and symbols that are most needful and appropriate for you will indeed come to and through you. Don't ever let the evil deeds of one person hold evil over good.

Signs and Symbols: The Misunderstood Gammadion

In informal speech, the words *sign* and *symbol* are often used interchangeably and roughly taken to mean the same thing. Given the charged nature of the symbol that came to me—the fire wheel technically known as a gammadion—some clarification is called for.

Even though the left-facing Buddhist or Bön gammadion predates the Nazis' use of the right-facing "swastika" version by thousands of years, it is obviously still a controversial symbol. There are, in fact, many different types of gammadions that have been used by many different spiritual and religious cultures throughout human history. The gammadion (or swastika) is a geometrical figure and a religious icon and a symbol of divinity and spirituality. In the Western world it was a symbol of auspiciousness and good luck until the 1930s, when it became a symbol of the Nazi and was then stigmatized by association with ideas of racism and anti-Semitism.

So, while the gammadion is certainly a symbol of an ancient tradition, for me, it was also a personally channeled sign—that is, feedback from the universe. When I first drew it as a small child, well, that was a sign about my future, and as you will see later in my story, it would reveal itself again as a sign of confirmation that I was literally on the correct path, even though that path was about to greatly deviate in ways I could not anticipate.

Bad News and Good News

The bad news is that most people—especially when they are in the second season—really are asleep, living unhappy waking-dream lives bounded by their five-sense experience. From the shamanic perspective, saying "most people are asleep"—literally not here—means that they wake up and go to work (A), then come home and watch TV (B), occasionally go on vacation or have some fun to mix things up a little bit kind of like a brief commercial break (C)—and then repeat the previous steps. Diagrammatically, their lives look something like this:

$$A \rightarrow B \rightarrow A \rightarrow B \rightarrow C \rightarrow A \rightarrow B \rightarrow A \rightarrow B \rightarrow C \rightarrow A \rightarrow B \rightarrow A$$

Over time, as these routines imprint our external lives and internal biology, we dig ourselves into some deep ruts. Our external ruts appear as work, family, and financial obligations. Our internal ruts are the well-worn neurological pathways in our brains. Like a river following the path of least resistance, as our repetitive thoughts and behaviors strongly flow through us, they create ever-deepening channels that make it easy to endlessly repeat ourselves.

Ultimately, we can become like children who have been traveling in a canoe down a river, back and forth with the tides. The river has worn the banks so tall that the children can no longer see the horizon. The only view is the river and its banks. It is all they know. And so they paddle each day to work and back, over and over again.

What's even worse is that for most people, neither A nor B are exciting, thrilling, fun, or otherwise in alignment with what they truly desire, who they really are, or why they are here. We are so busy striving and driving that we have dismissed the idea of being here for a reason. And in far too many cases, we have even forgotten how to naturally and spontaneously enjoy relaxed time with friends and family. Relaxing is hard—we are addicted to our screens—and politics and capitalism show us the underlying dis-ease that has been festering just beneath the surface for so very long.

> " Dis-ease of the mind, body, or spirit is merely a growth bump on the road to power. It is a gift, but only if one is willing to open the package.

We are a land of sleepwalkers suffering in quiet desperation and frustration, endlessly repeating ourselves, unaware of or unable to pursue our soul's true calling, and very much unaware that this is the state we are in. Not only do we become numb to how unhappy we are, we become numb to the possibility that things don't have to be—and weren't mean to be—this way. Even the thought of asking ourselves what are dreams and why we are here feels like an irresponsible and foolhardy task.

One day, however, we might catch a glimpse of something more or hear a gentle whisper calling to a different possibility. "Look, over there, are those signs leading us back to the meaning of our hot spots?" But then comes the critical question: When we catch that glimpse or hear the whisper, will we already be too far gone? Imprisoned by our routines and obligations in an all-too-often half-hearted and joyless waking dream, will we be aware enough or daring enough to experience and respond to the whisper, the possibility, the call? Can you hear it?

When we see or experience a thrilling serendipity, a stupendous synchronicity, or simply moments of pure and undeniable signs, will we even be available enough to notice what we have experienced and to follow up in the direction we have been pointed? Will we be able to remember enough of what we have seen or heard so that we will follow up with genuine action? Will we hold true to our experience of things when others beat it down as being "way out there" or just plain wacky?

❝ What you think of me is none of my business.

The good news? If you are reading these words, you have already taken a substantial step toward waking up. You have moved past any initial resistance to the pragmatic ancient wisdom worldview being espoused here, and something inside of you is now considering what the secrets of the seasons might mean for you, personally, as well as for your family, your loved ones, and the world at large.

Here's some more good news: As hard as some aspects of being alive turn out to be, it's also ultimately simply and natural—although not always easy in real time—to see the signs that are sent for you, to immerse yourself in the possibilities of your soul, and to awaken to a new and better life (which, often as not, requires no major external changes). As master David Chandler once said to me, "If it isn't simple, make it easy, and if it isn't easy, make it simple."

Domestication: Thinking Inside and Outside of Little Boxes and Big Boxes

It's important to see that the domestication process of the second season applies not just to our physical lives and our attempts to fit into the world and the kinds of places where we often end up living—especially if we are young, poor, oppressed, marginalized, or substantially different from the norm but to the very way we think. Essentially, in an effort to survive in our fast and overstimulated, externally powered, focused world, we make boxes—first little boxes and then big boxes—so we can divide up and separate all of this stimulation into neat, orderly containers.

Put differently, to deal with the magnitude of inputs and demands that our modern world impresses upon us, we begin this process of thought or object separation. But in doing this, we begin a process that results in further alienating ourselves from our world. That is, by dividing whole things into boxes, we are practicing the act of unconsciously training ourselves to believe in the dream of separation—and not just as a utility. We end up confusing the functional, practical act of dividing things up in the world with how we view ourselves and the world in the larger sense. (Some progressive Christian sources directly equate separation and sin, and the extremely popular *A Course in Miracles* tells us that in many ways, our belief in separation is our only problem.)

Like all forms of domestication, this destructive dream also begins in a subtle and innocent way that is supported by the utility of separating things out and then reinforced by seeing everyone else doing it. With enough practice, this way of thinking begins to carve deep neurological pathways that impact our inherent ability to see and process the truth—that we are all one and deeply interconnected. Our innocent act of utility-based dreaming turns this separation into a reality, envelopes our way of being, and expands through our culture to bring us the collective capitalistic, environmental, and political nightmares fueling the destruction of our species and the world we love.

Moving Beyond Our Diminished, Domesticated, Five-Sensory Delusion

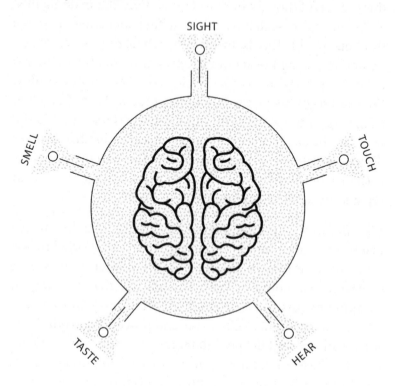

Let's reconsider the ubiquitous five-sensory delusion we find ourselves trapped in. For many people, the equivalent of five royal guards control access to the kingdom of the inner self. These guards—the five ordinary senses—constantly reinforce the societally broadcast message that unless you can see, hear, smell, touch, or taste something, it isn't real, doesn't affect the world, and shouldn't be taken seriously or acted upon.

Being asleep—the deluded and diminished state far too many people fall into and remain stuck in—can in part be attributed to the way we have been taught, trained, and reinforced to experience the five senses and deny everything else. This delusional, narcissistic five-sensory dream has, in effect, dulled and domesticated many of us, turned us away from the majesty of creation and our role in it, and tamed us to stop looking for, listening to, and becoming aware of and acting upon the signs, symbols, initiations, subtle energy, and general guidance being sent to us by the universe beyond the capacity of the rational mind and its five senses.

Such deep-seated conditioning keeps far too many people trapped in a fish bowl, sentenced to a joyless myopic life, plodding through time as they silently wonder whether this is all there is.

However, this is not even close to all there is, or all of who we are—not by a long shot. First, the notion that our brain is all of who we are is simply delusional: We are no more just our brains than we are our hearts or our livers. These may all be essential parts of our bodies, but they are not all of who we are.

Second, the notion that if something can be experienced, it must come through the five senses is flat-out delusional. The five senses cannot capture the reality of the soul or the majesty of the interconnected living universe, nor can our senses give us access to the information, feelings, and visions that originate within or are otherwise accessible only to the soul's mind.

Furthermore, taken just on their own terms, the five senses and the mind have built-in perceptual limitations. For example, we all know that a dog can hear frequencies much higher than we are capable of hearing. Just because we cannot hear the dog whistle, does that mean that sound does not exist? Of course not. The same is true for the limitations of senses that we have not yet developed or that we have forgotten even exist. Also, the mind by necessity selects what it pays attention to and, by doing this, eliminates from the conscious mind much that is around us every day.

Consider, then, the possibility that there is another sense. This is a sense that can be activated by believing in and attuning to our soul's mind, as well as by simply noticing that the interconnected living, loving universe is constantly sending us guidance. This sixth sense, however, is different from the rest of our senses. It is not a single-purpose narrow-band searchlight, but a portal to a rich, multidimensional world of magical connection, purpose, joy, and power.

Saying No to a 100-Year-Old Tai Chi Master

It was an ordinary Connecticut spring day; the promise of summer was in the air as the buds on the trees opened to the rain and obscured my windshield. I made my way up the steep, winding driveway that led to an old stone mansion, the home of my tai chi master, David Chandler.

When I was eleven or twelve, at a church rummage sale, I had bought a thin little paperback book with a white cover and black writing about the martial art of jujitsu. Many nights as I went to bed, my eyes would search for the book that rested between my child's Bible and Charles Dickens's dreaded *A Tale of Two Cities*. It brought me a strange but familiar sense of comfort, a hot spot I would come back to time and time again, both as a child and young adult.

It wasn't until a couple of years after college—fifteen years after I bought that book—that I attended my first martial arts class: tai chi. Over time I managed to fit tai chi in between my work and play and, seven years later, I was becoming an accomplished student in a martial art where there were no belts or levels to measure one's success.

My master was hosting a very special guest, Dr. Duang, an accomplished and aged teacher who had obtained a special visa and been sponsored to travel from China to teach and display his ancient martial art lineage. While he was giving many demonstrations across the state, a good forty dedicated tai chi and qi gong members came to this particular two-hour demonstration. I had read the usual tales one might expect to hear about ancient masters like Dr. Duang— throwing people across the room without touching them, or sending fire-like chi blasts through an opponent's body that reverberated for days after.

I hung on his every move as he walked into the center of the room. He could not speak a word of English, but his words were not what I was here for. He fit my vision of the look and feel of a legendary master and seer—an arched-over old man with a long pointy beard. He peered out of his tiny narrowed eyes and looked right into me as we were introduced. I was told he was 106 years old, but I couldn't believe it and simply dismissed the age as an inflated legendary tale.

When he began his demonstration, my chattering hyperactive mind went completely silent, and my entire body began to tickle from the inside out. His movements were slow and calculated, with no beginning or end, one motion seamlessly flowing into the next. His eyes shone like a tractor beam, carving through everything they touched—not tiger eyes or sleepy eyes, but a balanced gaze right down the middle.

I was deeply moved by his demonstration, even though no one got thrown across the room and Dr. Duang did not levitate. I was slightly disappointed but not surprised that I did not witness magic storybook maneuvers. Perhaps all of that was just a wishful fantasy.

At the end of the evening Dr. Duang's interpreter and assistant announced he would be conducting healing sessions for a few days and that if we wanted to sign up, we better do it fast as the spots were nearly filled. I signed up right away and took the first slot available, which was the second spot on his first day at 8:30 a.m.

Soon after I arrived for my 8:30 session, I heard my tai chi master say, "It's almost your turn. Time to go up." My stomach swirled as I walked up the winding open staircase with wrought iron rails and turned right into a small bedroom with a massage table standing all alone in the middle of the room. The first patient that day—a physician with a chronic bad back who had traveled a few hours to be there—brushed past me on his way out. He glanced at me with straight shooting eyes that reflected his crooked painful walk.

Entering the room a few minutes later, Dr. Duang's assistant told me to lie down on the table faceup. Dr. Duang laid his hands on my ankles. I lifted my chin and tightened my stomach muscles into an ever so slight crunch so I could peer out through the top of my eyes to see what this old man was about to do.

A tremendous impulse to laugh rose through me like an emotional rocket. It took every ounce of energy I could muster to hold it back. The man was a legend and had come from the other side of the world to share his noble gift with us. I swallowed back the urge to laugh with all my might, like I used to sometimes have to do sitting in a church pew as a young boy with my parents.

Dr. Duang increased his force as my resistance grew. He seemed completely aware of what was happening, like he was somehow enjoying playing with me or taunting me. Then all at once it became too much to handle—I broke down into a full roaring laugh as his hands moved up to my knees. I meant no disrespect, really, but I just couldn't help it and could not stop laughing.

After what seemed like five minutes of uncontrolled laughter, I opened my eyes to face the ancient teacher at my feet. I saw a grin on his face so large that it lifted the point of his beard toward his chin.

For the next fifty minutes he and I laughed hysterically as his hands danced across my body from side to side in a pattern that seemed well rehearsed. When he finished, I no longer had any cares or concept of time, and my abdomen felt like I had done two hundred sit-ups.

Dr. Duang mumbled something to his assistant, and then the two were clearly carrying on a conversation about me as their tone and tempo began to rise. They weren't laughing. Was I sick? Did he find something? Or perhaps I disrespected him with all of my laughter? My thoughts rushed to technology, financial calculations, and sales pipelines. In an hour I would be back in the city doing something that made sense. Or so I thought.

The assistant finally said, "Dr. Duang would like you to stay and assist him from now on."

"What do you mean from now on?" I asked, still reeling from the experience.

The assistant helped me off the table, directed me to Dr. Duang's side, and said, "He would like you to start, now."

For the next two days I worked next to Dr. Duang as he grunted and spoke in his native tongue to the assistant who then interpreted for me. Dr. Duang would have me place my hands on a patient in a way that exactly mirrored the placement of his own hands. While his movements were easy to follow, it was not the placement of the hands but what was supposed to be coming from the hands that really mattered.

Dr. Duang would ask the assistant to ask the patient if they were feeling anything from his hands. Each time the patients would respond by saying, "Oh yes." Then, as if to taunt me, he would have the interpreter ask the same question about my hand placements, and invariably the patient would say something like "No" or "Not really." Dr. Duang would look up at me straight in the eyes and grunt in disgust.

After this happened with a few patients, instead of grunting in disgust he reached out and slapped me on the cheek, with a playful loving energy of a zen master, and began to laugh hysterically.

At the end of the second day I was asked to have lunch with Dr. Duang, my tai chi master, and the assistant. A few bites into a dumpling, the assistant spoke up. "Dr. Duang would like to ask you something. He would like you to come back to China with him and assist him and be his apprentice for three months. Can you come?"

I laughed in response. "Are you kidding?"

He was not amused, and I quickly saw that he was dead serious. I politely explained that my family and professional obligations would not allow me to do such a thing. The tenor of the lunch changed, indicating that I had somehow disrespected the ancient master.

As I drove back down the winding driveway, I felt a familiar sinking feeling in my stomach as a massive breeze of emotions swept through me. Had I just walked away from something that was supposed to be an important part of me? No, I convinced myself. Even thinking about following a strange old man to China to seriously explore this foreign style of medicine was folly. I had a family to support and take care of and many clients and others who relied on me.

By the time I reached the road I was happily thinking about work and no longer aware of the ache in my stomach. Somewhere inside of me—somewhere far beyond my ordinary five senses—I knew that a fish had just surfaced from a still pond and sent out many ripples. Because I had turned down Dr. Duang's request, the surface was once again smooth, but I did not consider at what expense.

Time: The Tricky Inconstant Constant of Our Lives

Our experience of the seasons, as mentioned earlier, is not linear—in fact, far from it. We experienced ever-lasting love and wonder in the first season, our knowledge of our soul—of who we are—providing us with a rich tapestry of love that lasts a lifetime and serves as our saving grace and anchor when things turn tough.

When we look back on the events of season two, it often seems that time has flown by incredibly quickly. Similarly, when we look to the future, it seems incredibly far away, as if we will never get there.

The point here is that it is *only* when we become fully present with time—when we look the light of our lives right in the eye—that time feels just right. Then we can fully accept the moment where we are—right here, right now—and be fully present to both our past and our future.

It's also important to see and feel time in the big moments of our lives, the ones that shape us and leave hot spots, the ones that present us with a road we might have walked down but didn't. Had I said yes to Dr. Duang, my entire life might have been very different. That possible future, embedded in the moment I turned him down, was never to come to pass, but the lessons that it contained were sure to come back to me in other ways.

How a Zebra Built a Business among a Herd of Horses

" A tree doesn't try to grow and woodpeckers don't get sore necks.

For most of my life, I looked and lived the part of the typical guy who grows up to become a financial consultant and entrepreneur. Notwithstanding some of the unusual events and experiences I had, from the outside, my childhood looked much like anyone else's. I was raised in a small town in the northeast United States. My father was a scientist, pragmatic and conservative. My mother was a teacher who left her job to raise my two sisters and me. My family attended church every Sunday. I liked the morals, but not the dogma. I was an excellent athlete, but for the most part, the school curriculum bored me.

A few years after graduating from college, I made an important career choice: to become a financial advisor. Looking around it became clear that money controlled most people's lives, and I felt it should be the other way around. I got married and bought a house, and the postman backed up a truck into the driveway to deliver my financial exams study materials.

The countless hours of focused study at the hardwood dining room table had irritated my right elbow from leaning on it for so long leaving me with a wound that had to be treated. But nothing could hold me back from my new mission of helping people with their money.

I passed the tests and was ready to take on the world in my new financial advisor role. This was a profession that would enable me to help people now while building toward the dream I had always had of opening my own healing center on a warm-water island—a dream I'll return to shortly. Since it was not my nature to work for a big Wall Street firm, I went out on my own after some brief mentoring from an independent advisor.

Looking back through my seasons, I can see now that thanks to my second season of "doing" and trying to be really "something," I was trying to make myself into something special instead of *me* as I worked very hard at my career to make everyone love me.

Each day I would not allow myself to eat lunch until I helped three new people with their money and retirement. My goal was six new clients per day, so I reasoned that I needed to hit the halfway mark by noon. Many nights I would come home worn and hungry. I was fueled by my dream and my sense of purpose in helping my clients to achieve financial freedom.

Just five hard, short years later I had made it to the top of the sales production charts with unprecedented rapid growth. I had secured an in-demand niche: a caring financial advisor who took the time to educate and service clients the way that they deserved to be treated. Soon I was adding more staff and another advisor to the team. The clients loved us and we loved them.

Our vendors also loved us as well, with big names like Fidelity, Pimco, Citigroup, Franklin Templeton, and Janus as our go-to products. Working in the investment world had its privileges, including going to exotic locations for conventions sponsored by the vendors.

We were high up in the Canadian mountains at a famous resort hotel where I stood backstage at this conference with the executive team and the other top advisors. We were about to be paraded in front of a few thousand top advisors as being one of the top ten vendors of a particular product, made possible by my having grown my team's business to over 2,000 clients.

With drink in hand, I stood there by myself as the other nine advisors mingled together. I was feeling proud and awkward, enjoying the resort environment but feeling desperately out of place. I pretended not to care that I was not part of the group and started up a conversation with someone passing out hors d'oeuvres. That's when the other nine honorees turned together and meandered over to where I was standing.

The apparent leader moved close enough so I could smell the whiskey on his breath, and he said: "Hey, kid, tell me. What's your secret? How did you make it here so fast?"

Responding in my natural, authentic, undefended manner, I matter-of-factly replied, "No secret, my team and I just love every single client."

They all walked away, all at once, without making a sound. And in that moment, I knew for certain that I was a zebra in a herd of horses.

The Full Nelson Incident: A Business Stolen

Despite advice from some more experienced financial advisors, I continued to outspend my competition on service. One month we had over four hundred boxes of chocolates going out to clients for birthday presents. I was in it for the long run, razor-focused on my goals, and dedicated to truly caring for each and every client. Keeping a grinding pace over the next few years, I quietly became more anxious, feeling that life's expanding obligations were somehow swallowing up the reality of my deepest dreams.

Life went on. By my thirties I was living in a large house in Connecticut with a swimming pool overlooking the Long Island Sound. Married, with two amazing children, two boats, two Mercedes, and a nanny who had become a special part of our lives. I continued to practice tai chi and be the best dad I knew how to be to my beautiful kids.

On the outside, life was good, but on the inside, well, some mornings I would wake up in a full sweat, terrified I would forget my dreams and lose touch with the why—the why I was here on this earth. Life marched on and the rumbles of my soul were temporarily muted with the warm blanket of external success.

Family was the most important thing to me. A wonderful family life had been modeled for me—my adoptive mother and father, and my two sisters, were the best family anyone could have ever asked for. But my own marriage was now proving to be a challenge. Home was not a place of rest. My responsibilities for the care of my children were increasing as the situation at home deteriorated. At night I'd tuck my kids into bed and remind them that they each had a special gift, and their job was to find that gift and let it shine throughout the world.

But I wasn't really doing this myself. I was struggling with the feeling that there was more and knew that I needed to get to it, but felt as if I was running with an anchor around my neck. Something was definitely holding me back. To some significant degree, I felt like a fraud.

Life seemed to have consumed me and was threatening to take my dreams away with it. I felt desperate, angry, and trapped as I smiled throughout my days with my game face on. On the outside I was playing the role of a successful, confident businessman, while on the inside I felt more and more out of control. The standard cocktail party question, "What do you do?" made me increasingly uncomfortable and became harder and harder to answer.

That's when it all began to fall apart.

I was on another vendor-sponsored trip, this one at a five-star resort in the South. During the second day of festivities the senior manager of the sponsoring company sent one of his "men" over to me while I was sipping on a rum drink:

"There is a special trip happening tomorrow and you're invited if you'd like to come."

Filled with pride at being selected as part of a special elite group, I naturally agreed. We were going to be taken to a private deserted island for a day of lobster and libations, with only a handful of special advisors being invited.

The next morning, a well-equipped shiny black private coach pulled up through the parade of tall palms. Drinks were served before I could even sit down. Thirty minutes later we pulled down a dirt road where a large two-story pontoon boat was docked. As we boarded, we were escorted to the top deck and offered more cocktails from the open bar.

Relaxing music played in the background as the senior executive came up beside me. I felt sure he had an agenda—the top power executives always did. I wondered, "Why me?" He was positioning himself to command everyone's attention. He was at the top of his game with one of the most powerful corporations in the world and was not shy about his appetite for power and his aspiration to be on top.

With all eyes on him, he took my drink from my hand and passed it off to the nearest person. Then he walked behind me and slid his right arm up underneath my right arm as his hand reached up and settled on the back of my neck.

"Half nelson," he shouted, invoking the move of a wrestler.

The crowd's anxious chatter suddenly hushed. All I could hear were the screeches of cunning seagulls flying by and looking for a meal. He then jammed his left arm up under my left arm, resting his hand on my neck, mirroring the exact position of his right arm.

"Full nelson," he said.

He was now hidden behind me, in complete control. I was alone, looking out at the complicit and smiling crowd. With both palms now firmly on the back of my neck, with fingers tightly locked and his muscular hairy arms forcing my relatively scant arms up toward my ears, he shouted: "Father Nelson!"

Invoking the infamous priest who was caught molesting children, this powerful corporate executive began to thrust his hips back and forth from behind. The crowd went wild with laughter as I felt his hot breath on my neck and his body uncomfortably close to mine. My only external response was to mirror the gawking crowd with an awkward smile.

I continued to the island with a smile on my face—my game face—and kept it there the remainder of the trip.

It was rumored that I was to be offered an executive position at this firm and to be prepared for this discussion if it arose. The following day this top executive invited my wife and me to the beach to spend some one-on-one time with him and his wife. Without hesitation, I politely declined. In an instant, he turned his head and walked away.

A few weeks later I was asked to come to company headquarters. I sat at a small round conference table with the executive who directly reported to my Father Nelson antagonist. I had come to think of this fellow as a friend, but as I watched him fidget like a new gang member going through an initiation by having to off someone, I quickly realized I had a big problem.

"We are going to exit this market," he said, "so your business is going to be sold."

My stomach sank and everything went silent, including me. I was still in the room, but not really present. A half smile came to my lips as my head swirled for options and exit strategies. I pushed back with a couple of light remarks, but when his face remained serious and stern, it quickly became evident that this was no joke. After a few more moments of silence, I fired back with a sharp challenge to his ridiculous statement suggesting that somehow he had the authority to tell me what to do with my business.

"If I were you, I might get legal counsel," he said. "But know this. You would end up spending years in a battle with one of the most powerful corporations in the world. Not a good move in my opinion."

I had put my heart, blood, and soul into building a business that I expected would take care of my clients, my family, and my dream for the rest of my life. Suddenly I was facing a situation that was taking it all away. Even now, it's difficult to remember my exact words, but in essence I calmly stated that I would get counsel and asked about any other ways to make this work.

"I can't believe how well you are taking this," he said.

Although none of this was apparent to me at the time, it's remarkable how uncomfortably similar the two of us were in that meeting. Although we were coming from very different places, he was incapable of having any emotional connection to my pain, a personality trait that served him well in the corporate world. And I was incapable of connecting to the depth of my own emotions, which was serving me well living an average ordinary domesticated moderate life with my soul wound tucked safely out of sight.

And that soul wound was either going to remain tucked away and carry me through a mediocre life or erupt through my veins and awaken me.

Throughout the next six months, this mega-corporation played me like an innocent child. One day I was getting additional business and it was all just a big mistake. The next day I was tempted with the promise of a big sale that would make me happy. It was probably a game to keep me from digging too deep with legal counsel and to keep me spending my money on running the business so that, when the day came, there would be minimal disruption resulting in a smooth sale and transition. The downside of being raised in a family with strong moral values is that I was sheltered from many of the harsh realities of the world, which proved to be a liability in the business world.

This mega-corporation was my largest and primary vendor, and legal counsel advised me that even though I did not work for them, they "kind of" had the right to do this based on the fine print buried deep in the contract I had signed with them. And they really could tie things up for years, leaving me battered and penniless. So, it was best to take whatever amount they would offer, which in the end amounted to a tiny fraction of what my book of business was worth.

I was crushed and in a complete state of shock. I felt lost, with nowhere to go. All of my doing was taken away from me in a single shattering episode, and because I had fallen into the conventional domesticated dream of trying to achieve a certain kind of success, I felt like I was dying.

A part of my life was over—my dream was gone—and there was simply nothing I could do about it. Yes, as a survivor, I knew that I would have to find a way to move on and that I would indeed find that way. But the truth is that on the inside I felt like I was completely falling apart. In the long run, I can now see that this prepared me so well for where I was going, but at the time, it felt like a big piece of me had died.

A Lifelong Dream: Islands of Sanity with Centers of Healing

5

*Spirit whispers to us in the gaps between our thoughts,
in the space between the notes, in the pause between the
breaths; take the courage to sit for a while and say ... hi!*

Ever since I can remember, I'd had a specific dream. Like any dream, it had taken on different flavors over the years. The core ingredients, however, always remained the same: By age forty, I would have a place of my own where people could come to step away from the busyness of life to remember why they were here, and to find the power and courage to live their dreams and passionately embrace life.

One day in college "that place" became clear. I was off on a spring break trip with two buddies. We sailed out of Miami through Biscayne Bay into the middle of the thick black night. Powerboats with no lights buzzed past our bow.

"Drug runners," said the captain. "They won't bother us, now that they've let us know who's boss."

When the sun rose the next morning, I knew I had found the home of my dreams. I was in another world. The water was green and pure, and the beauty of the deserted islands I saw exceeded anything I'd ever imagined. I wondered why everyone in the world didn't live here. This was the place I had been dreaming of my whole life. Here is where I was to build my healing center, where people could get away from the madness and busyness of life and remember how to fully live their dreams.

Later on, after I built my financial advisory business, the daily demands of running it—and keeping up with my other activities and studies—had substantially increased. I would often find myself wistfully looking at the map of the Caribbean islands that hung prominently in the back operations office, just above the copy machine, and take solace in my dream.

Each year my written goals would begin like this: "Build a place in the islands where people can come to get away and remember why they are here, to live a life of passion and purpose."

An Extraordinary Unexpected Ordinary Teacher

As I kept up a grinding pace building my business, I quietly became more anxious, feeling that life's expanding obligations were swallowing up the reality of my dream. One day I met up with an old school friend—someone who knew me well—at a local restaurant. What he said disturbed me.

"I don't get it. Why are you spending your life doing this, when you want to do that? That's just stupid. Why don't you just go follow your island dream?"

At that point in my life I was not awake enough to acknowledge the feeling of discomfort that I felt in my body when a teacher was present telling me something I was not ready to hear. As I would much later realize, teachers appear all the time in many forms; it is the student who must be present to hear the lesson.

I glanced up at the TV above his shoulder as a way of avoiding this ordinary teacher who sat in front of me. All I could feel was the whirling of my brain and the barking of my voice as I blustered about how ridiculous his assessment was.

My family, mortgage, and other worldly demands had no rational place for such logic. Still, inside myself, I felt the truth in what he was saying. Driving out of the parking lot, I plotted the afternoon's schedule, took a deep breath, and felt more invested than ever in my resolution to do the responsible thing and build toward my dream with a solid foundation of financial stability.

I then spent the next few years working my tail off so I could prosper and then make my healing center dream a reality. During my busy workdays, people would often tell me that they wanted to put away as much money as they could if it would allow them to get out of their job and begin to live. I would feel pity for these people as I saw them sacrificing so much of the present life for some future dream. I wondered how many people would even make it to their dream—how many would get sick or die first, and how many would get to retirement only to forget their dream?

It made me tremendously sad to watch these people spend every day of their lives doing something they didn't like. Money seemed to dominate everything in their lives. My own dream, I thought, well, it made sense to put that off for now because

I was building to it. But these other people, they were really missing life's boat. I would eventually find that the lessons that came from hiding my gifts and not being in my power would later return to me in ways I could have never imagined.

After my business was lost—as described in the last chapter—I was paralyzed with fear and shock, my pride and sense of stability gone—just like that.

I spent the next months in a numbed state of fear moving throughout the days with my game face on. Each day I sat in a room in my home looking over Long Island Sound, in a controlled panic. Out my window to my right I watched my kids enjoy our beautiful pool while I did everything to look and feel productive. From my view straight ahead I could see the distant shores of New York across the water.

I hustled to find something to rescue my huge financial loss; time in between helped me to become more conscious that my worlds were beginning to collide—my need to work with spirit and energy, and my desire to help people with finances, corporations, and the capital markets—and that it was becoming increasingly difficult to keep them separate. Throughout the country the gap between the rich and poor was widening, just like the gap between my business life and my spiritual life.

On the one hand I was disgusted with the business world and angry about my still fresh wound. On the other hand, I still hungered for the illusive feeling of money and security, and desperately hung on to my dream of building a healing center and doing energy medicine work in the Caribbean. I picked up my tattered version of Steven Mitchell's *Tao Te Ching* and the not-really-random page I turned to read:

> *Fill your bowl to the brim and it will spill. Keep sharpening your knife and it will blunt. Chase after money and security and your heart will never unclench. Care about*

people's approval and you will be their prisoner. Do your work, then step back. The only path to serenity.

Really Hot Spots: Healing Reminders Handed over at a Blistering Pace

 Don't believe everything you think.

You have a reason for being here. Even if your reason seems strange to some (including you), or doesn't make sense or fit into your culture, religion, or family ideals, it is your duty—ultimately your *raison d'être* (reason for being)—to find a way to uncover and follow it. This is where true self-knowledge and courage start; this is where the first step of the warrior's path that we are all on begins.

Long before my business was stolen, I would on occasion allow myself to break away for a daylong or weekend class or event on spirituality or energy medicine. But when I did, strange things would happen—like touching someone and detecting an unknown health problem, or clearly seeing and articulating a core but hidden psychological issue that was tearing someone apart. Essentially, as soon as I allowed myself to break free from the conventional reality shackles that bound me, synchronicities would arise landing me in situations that would provide me with the opportunity to give back this mysterious gift to others.

One example stands out. After one tai chi class, I gently touched the upper chest of a woman (in an appropriate place) whom I had previously gotten to know well through attending classes together. The moment I touched her, she immediately turned white. She said my touch felt electric and wanted to know what

I had done. When I asked her how her heart was, she began to cry. She eventually told me she had gone to the doctor who was concerned and needed to do more tests. Needless to say it was a bit awkward, and I really didn't know what to say or do.

Over the next few months, as similar incidents kept occurring, I eventually decided that it was all just too odd and out of place, and none of it had any place in my life. I decided to stop reaching out, embracing, and touching others.

But as soon as I did that—within a couple of days—my own hands turned on me as angry red blisters bubbled up from underneath my skin. As I looked at and felt the blisters—for which there was no ordinary explanation—I vividly found myself going back to my high school automobile accident, the feeling of the presence that helped me hold on, and the sense that I had been saved because I was here for a reason.

It soon became clear to me that the presence that saved me— which by then I sometimes thought of as my guides—had made a deal with me: *You have been given a very special gift. We will not allow you to ignore it. It is your destiny to use your gifts in many ways to benefit and give back to others.*

Apparently, something inside and perhaps outside of me cared enough to do whatever it took to wake me up vis-à-vis my gifts and my responsibility for developing and using them. I had a deep feeling that if I did not want to have this something bequeath me with a crisis or major illness to motivate me, I would need to pay attention and act on these signs and feelings.

By this point the blisters on my hands had become uncomfortable sores that made almost perfect circles around each of my palms. Again, I got a deep sense and feeling of gratitude that it was only blisters and not something life threatening. Ever since I was a little kid, I had always said a silent prayer to lead me to power in my life and to guide and teach me whatever I needed to do to live in accordance with my purpose.

As I grew older and wiser, I added the notion of "with compassion" to that regularly used silent prayer. Essentially, then, I had made a deal with whatever part of me I thought could hear and respond to my situation: I would do more intuitive, healing, and empowerment work with people, and, in exchange, the blisters and sores would go away. And that's just what happened.

Something life altering was happening as I began to open up to and work with the existence of subtle energies. Out of complete faith in following whatever it was that was opening up inside me, I enrolled in a three-year master's course in energy medicine, led by a gifted woman named Dr. Dorothy.

In my second year of the program, I finally mustered up my courage to follow my dreams and longings and decided to move with my family to the Caribbean islands. I would live on St. John, a small beautiful island filled with beautiful people. While I lived there, I had a thriving practice doing my empowerment work at a famous resort for a wealthy and externally powerful clientele.

The work I provided was a combination of energy medicine and intuitive empowerment coaching that grew and advanced my skills in helping people move into their authentic power and live in expanded consciousness and peak performance. During this time I would commute from the islands to the mainland to attend to business matters and continue my coursework and programs at the institute.

Getting the Sign to Go to Nepal

I loved my home and my life on the island of St. John. I felt so good about living and following my dreams and, for the first time ever, living in a place that felt like home. But there was trouble brewing in paradise.

My marriage wasn't good; it hadn't been good for years, but things were coming to a head. I was changing and growing, which was putting stress on some of my relationships. When anyone chooses to become more of who he or she really is, many of the people originally attracted into that person's life will go into a semi-panic. We are creatures of habit, change is uncomfortable to our species, and the closer the relationship, the bigger the challenge.

My parents had a fabulous relationship and marriage. But in my case, the splitting of a primary relationship had to take place for the good of everyone involved, including both parents and their children.

Life continued on the island with new friends, late afternoon snorkels, kids chasing lizards, early evenings "riding the rail" at the Quiet Mon for an after-work drink, and early morning rush down the mountain to drop off the kids to catch the boat for school. Each month I would continue to fly back to the mainland for a weekend of classes at the energy medicine institute I attended.

One time on my way back to school, I stood at the edge of the cement dock saying goodbye to my family as the ferry blew its horn. Before hustling through the gate, I turned one last time to hug my beautiful seven-year-old son, and as I turned to hug my nine-year-old daughter, I saw tears in her eyes.

"What's the matter, honey?" I asked. "You know Dad comes home in a few days."

"I know," she said, "but each time you go, you come back different."

As I sat on the upper deck, I looked back to see my family drive up the mountain and marveled at the wisdom of my little daughter. The school I attended and the work I was doing was helping me transform. I was sad for the losses that lingered and those that were ahead, but also glad for my growth.

The horn blew as the boys untied the thick rope that held the ferry on the dock and tossed it ashore. A puff of thick black smoke filled the pure blue air, and I thought back to the words of my tai chi master: "With every gain, there is a loss, as with every loss, there is a gain."

In that moment I knew I would not be able to hold things together much longer—I was exhausted, and my kids deserved better. It was one of the hardest things I would ever have to do, but I knew that now was the time.

I didn't realize how bad the separation would hurt. I didn't know how difficult it would be to keep myself from slipping back into complacency, from pretending that things were really not that bad, and from convincing myself that I should just keep moving in step with the conditioned dance of my relationship that had brought me this far in life. I did not want to hurt anyone—my kids, my extended family, or my wife. I had a lot to think about on that flight home that night.

My trip to the mainland and back was uneventful, and the following month I headed back for another weekend of classes. A bonus class was held at the end of the weekend in the evening after school—a drumming circle led by Richard, one of the teachers. We sat in a circle as he talked about shamanism and strange practices such as journeying.

Richard banged a drum in rhythm and told us to think of things in our mind and to go someplace, like a cave, and sit there and wait for an animal to come to us. Then we were supposed to ask this animal if it was our power animal, our teacher. I thought this was somewhat ridiculous, but I did my best to imagine what he asked.

Soon the drum began to beat faster, which we had earlier been told was our cue to come out of the cave and back into the room—into our bodies. I thought back to my only connection to this type of experience and the term *shaman*. Freshman year in college, my favorite college professor had us read a book about a South American shaman and all of his crazy adventures. I loved my professor and knew he was taking a risk by having us read this kind of a book at a religious-based school. Something about that book and the anthropological teachings that semester touched me deeply, another hot spot waiting to be revealed.

Back in the room, Richard began to ask about people's experiences and if anyone wanted to share. After we heard a few stories from the other students about dancing dolphins and soaring eagles, he began to speak of a man who had taught him the ways of a shaman: Dr. Larry.

As he spoke the name of this shaman, I felt a deep stirring inside. I had come to befriend these feelings at this point in my growth, lessons that I was being given since early childhood. I began to quiet my rational mind and surrender to the moment. I knew what this kind of sign meant—pay attention and follow where it takes you. I sat up straight and took note of the name, Dr. Larry, so I would not forget it.

That evening, as I was retiring in my cozy and by now familiar hotel room, I looked out into the black of night as I always did and scanned the parked planes with darkened windows to see if I could pick out my ride for the next morning. The mere thought of flying back to my home in the islands sent a surge of joy through me.

Before I fell asleep, I opened my laptop, and a quick Google search found Dr. Larry without any problem. Without much thought, beyond the fact that California was three hours behind us, I picked up the phone and dialed the number.

"Hello, this is Carol," a woman said.

"Hi, my name is Larry, and I saw on your website that you guys sometimes do retreats, and I was wondering if you have anything happening in August?"

August was not far away. Fortunately, the terms of my pending divorce provided me—for the first time in my life—with an entire month to myself, which happened to be August.

"Well, how did you get our name?"

I told her that I had been given the name of Dr. Larry at an energy medicine program being offered by one of his students, who said that there were sometimes retreats.

"Well," she said, "we just happen to have a trip for the month of August to Nepal to train and initiate with some very special shamans. We are pretty full, but we could take one more person."

I had been praying for a sign to lead me to my next teacher, my next step, and this was now beginning to feel right.

"I'm in," I said without hesitation. "Sign me up." She chuckled and replied with some high-level details and some forms that I would have to fill out as to my background and experience.

That night I fell asleep longing for this adventure and questioning my rash decision to travel across the world to train with shamans and a man I knew almost nothing about.

Kathmandu ... But My Fate: To Do Not 6

Each day, each moment, I am growing—INTO my power,
my dreams ... that is why I am here.

I think I'm going to Kathmandu, I hummed Bob Seger's song about going to Kathmandu softly to myself.

I was sitting in coach class, on the tarmac in Connecticut, after connecting through a boat ride and plane trip from my island. On my way now to Kathmandu, I had time to reflect. I'd exchanged my laptop bag for my old worn backpack, and now I was ready to head to the other side of the world—to the other side of reality.

The old Bob Seger tune circled around my head over and over again. I found my mind groping for the sequence of logical reasons that had led me to be in an airplane on my way to Nepal to train for a month with and be initiated by indigenous shamans, leaving behind my career and monetary responsibilities, my children, and the wreckage of my marriage.

Many of my fellow travelers were on their cell phones while a wave of insignificance swept through my mind, adding to my already uncertain state.

"Excuse me, sir, are you heading home or just starting your business trip?"

The question asked by the bright-looking women in a dark suit sitting next to me completely stumps me. Now why would she think I was a businessman? I must have still been carrying a business man reality about me. I wondered if I would be asked the same question on my return.

It was a good question: Why wasn't I on a business trip? A business trip is safe, productive, and well understood in advance. I sit up straight as I face the truth—my own truth. I am going to Kathmandu because of a belief—a belief that messages and signs come to me in ways that I may not always understand, but when I trusted these knowings and followed the signs, while the path was not always easy, it was always correct.

I had been told that in Kathmandu, on the other side of the world, there existed a different way of expressing and regarding power than the external money-focus that always prevailed in the United States. For me, given my ongoing work as a financial advisor, it would be a happy and welcome change.

I pulled the airplane magazine from the seat pocket and moved my finger along the flight route. It took me a while to pinpoint Nepal on the global map. And speaking of maps, let me now lay out for you how, in retrospect, I had arrived at this particular juncture in time.

A Bird's-Eye View of Signs through My Seasons

The particular path I was now on arose from a confluence of sources. First, I had been training in expanded consciousness, subtle energies, and energy medicine for years now, and my particular abilities and proclivities seemed to match up with the kind of healing work that shamans had done for thousands of years. I often had a deep sense or knowing of what people needed; I had potent hands; and I was always guided to the heart of the matter of a person's challenge—or as the shamans call it the original place of the soul wound.

Second, a few months earlier, at a workshop at my energy medicine school, I heard the name "Dr. Larry" mentioned, which had sent a powerful shock through my system. When I learned that he was leading a shamanic initiation pilgrimage to Kathmandu at the exact same time I had a free month, I spontaneously, immediately signed up.

As the plane easily took off, I found my mind thinking back to another sign that had occurred just a few weeks before. Still on St. John, sitting on the deck of my house, I was gazing over the emerald sea when a distinct image flew into my mind of a person sitting in the corner of a dark cement room. I couldn't make out who it was, or what the person looked like, but then the person intentionally showed me his eyes. I could see those eyes perfectly, and it sent an exhilarating shock through my entire body.

I wondered if I'd been visited by someone. I was not dreaming because I was not sleeping. *I was not.* Could it really have been a visit from a shaman of some kind, or was I letting my coming adventure in Nepal go to my head?

Later in the day we went for a hike with my kids, up the "gut"—a beautiful stream with a magnificent mango tree about three quarters of the way up the mountain at a majestic fork in the brook. The kids were ahead of us and called out, "There's this amazing bird. Hurry up and look." I told them not to touch it, in a protective way, and as I hiked up, I saw this astounding bird—it was tall and had a build close to a heron, but wasn't one—standing on a rock very close to the mango tree. I had never seen a bird like that in St John, and to this day I still have not. Even when my kids got close, the bird didn't move.

I crawled over a large, smooth gray boulder and found a spot to sit while the water rushed past my bare feet. Then I looked into its eyes, this bird—somehow—had the same eyes that had visited me in my mind earlier in the day. After the kids continued their climb up the gut, I moved closer to the bird—about three feet away—and its eyes were *exactly* the same as the eyes I'd seen earlier that day. And I mean *exactly* the same, one thousand percent the same.

Part of me just said, "Come on, Lawrence, this is all crazy. It is nothing more than a coincidence. You are just making this into something you want it to be." But then I thought that if we came back later and this bird was still there, then perhaps it might really mean something.

When we returned an hour or so later, the bird was still there. I sent the kids ahead and sat close for maybe a half hour as it barely moved and looked right back into my eyes. My gaze softened in meditation, memorizing those eyes in exquisite detail, wondering about things beyond my ability to comprehend and if perhaps one day this may make sense.

Another Brick of the Call

Thirty-six hours and twelve meals later, the huge pink and purple plane lowered itself over a strange land with rolling green hills and box-like cement homes stacked on top of one another. Bright prayer flags hung across the rooftops, and huge white-tipped mountains laced the cloud-scattered horizon. I said a small prayer as we taxied toward the simple brick airport building overgrown with bush. Hustled by a swarm of young porters hungry for fresh American currency, I was reminded of the need to trust myself and my own worldly instincts on a trip such as this.

The non–air-conditioned bus—with windows mysteriously closed shut—looked like those I'd seen in *National Geographic*. It bounced over bumpy roads and was filled with small brown people in bright clothing jammed closely together, sweating.

We were on our way to see Ama Bombo (Mother Shaman), and I wondered what she would be like. Our pilgrimage leader and head guide, Dr. Larry, read my travel-weary face and said, "Don't even think about being tired. Ama Bombo gets up at 4:30 every morning and sees thirty to fifty patients each day— she is tireless. We must begin preparation for your initiation; there is much to do."

Waiting to see Ama Bombo, I caught a sneak preview of the towering statue that lay inside a mysterious, small-arched opening. The Boudhanath Stupa, like all stupas, is a sacred structure, a large outdoor temple, that embodies the essential elements and goals of both Tibetan Buddhist and Shamanic practice. It has thirteen steps or levels—leading to heaven— and at the top, Buddha's all-knowing eyes peered out in all four directions. I was filled with tingling emotion. Having heard of people having religious experiences when visiting such sacred places, I wondered if I was having one.

Haunting tinny sounds of prayer wheels spun endlessly; I pawed at them with my right hand and circumnavigated the stupa clockwise, one among hundreds. An old monk in torn

Converse high-tops passed by me as he mumbled, chanted, and fondled his prayer beads.

Three times around the stupa was said to bring enlightenment, but I was lost. I broke my trance and peered over my left shoulder to see three-story multicolored shops everywhere. Filled with spiritual wares for sale, they blocked the view of the mountains, but also acted as a kind of protective screen, isolating the sacred circular space of the stupa from the stench and poverty that lay outside the sacred gates of the Valley of Boudhanath. The ubiquitous smell of burning incense was a welcome relief.

Soon after, as I was being led up the steps into Ama Bombo's house, Shaman Ram, a guide, turned to me. "It takes you people forty years for your initiation, and then when you begin to experience it working you, you run away and call it a midlife crisis—very funny, very sad."

Ram's head barely reached the ribs of my six-foot-two frame, but I sensed his lofty power, which would later play a pivotal role in my journey. We entered Ama's home and walked over the assortment of soiled shoes that lay strewn outside the small dim room where she sat, chanting, an old worn cushioned armchair serving as her throne. She peered at me out of the corner of her eye; it felt as if we already knew each other, as if she could see right into my soul.

Dr. Larry turned to me and whispered, "We do not separate our spiritual life from our everyday life. Our shaman work often takes place right in the middle of our homes, just as our temples are often right in the middle of our streets."

For the next several days, I sat on a damp cement floor from seven in the morning until dusk, in the corner of the ten-by-twelve room. I watched sick babies, old women, monks, and teenagers waiting, then going inside to be healed.

Her energy was inexhaustible. Like an athlete who loses herself in the flow of a game, Ama was giving and teaching from the "well" without depleting herself. At times she was wrathful, grabbing hair and kicking away evil spirits. I waited for three whole days before I went forward to receive a healing.

"I am blessed with good health," I said. "I am here to ask for power, to fully open and become all that I am here to become in this lifetime." She told me my god is Kali, the deity she embodies, and gave me some special beads and a mantra.

"You have the gift," Ama said. Her hand was on my head as she shook and sent tremors throughout my body. When we were finished, I walked outside and noticed a broken brick lodged in the mud outside her door. *The brick was etched with the sign I had been seeing and drawing ever since fifth grade*—the gammadion, the Bön symbol that had come to me in my childhood. Something powerful and real was *definitely* happening.

Initiation

An important day for all shamans (and for the Hindu religion overall) is Janai Purnima, the full moon of the lunar month of Saun (July/August). Janai refers to the sacred yellow threads worn by high caste adult Hindu males that are changed on this holy day; Purnima means "day of the full moon." Janai Purnima marks the period when the deities return to rejuvenate their power (*sakti*). Obstacles and traps are often deliberately set by other shamans on this day to make sure one is worthy of such power.

"You must be impeccable," said Ama Bombo, with a deep look of concern in her eyes.

Thousands of small faces laced the walls of the loosely tangled buildings and echoed the cheers of "Se, se, se, se Bomba, se" ("dance, dance, dance, dance Shaman, dance"). I was dancing the shaman dance through villages, around temples, and down narrow alleyways on the way to Kumbaswar, the holy waters to gain power.

It was really happening—I was on my pilgrimage, my initiation, my Janai Purnima. My shaman dress billowed around my ankles while the bells hung from my shoulders, ringing out my path. My drum was held just the right way. I pounded in rhythm, all day, blisters appearing on my hands, and occasionally I glanced toward a seasoned shaman—checking my form.

Peacock feathers stood tall upon my head, connecting the rainbow bridge to the gods. My sweat-soaked dress became heavy, as did my thoughts. And it was still only morning. I vacillated between shame and pride, drudgery and bliss, exhaustion and power. In the eyes of most Americans, being or becoming a shaman was not understandable or acceptable (no less being a shaman, financial advisor, and business consultant at the same time). Here, the presence of shamans is the way of life.

I turned the corner of a smoky temple and paused to catch my breath. I bowed to a holy man. He looked at me and gestured for me to stand up. He then rose, folded his hands in prayer, and bowed. This was clearly the day of the shaman.

Later—it was dark and I had no idea how much time has passed—a ruddy stench began to enter my consciousness. I do not wear a watch and found myself encased in a timeless, small uncomfortable cement room. A surge of negativity washed through my sleepy, wobbly body and cloudy mind. I felt as though someone was turning a fire hose on me, blasting me with every possible weak thought and insecurity I had ever felt—or had ever even thought about feeling.

Like all good shamans, I had begged for power. *I thought I was supposed to become enlightened, empowered!* But now, I just wanted to go home. I was tired of dirt and poverty. And all of this spiritual growth and shamanic pilgrimaging felt crazy to me.

Fortunately, I told myself in a consoling inner voice, I would soon be going back to work, reserving the spiritual side of my life for a few hours a week on Sundays. Yes, I'd take it nice and easy, with only small, careful doses of introspection and spiritual seeking. I'd mow the lawn, pay the bills, attend to the family, and consume myself with money and earning status—activities that felt safe and that I and everyone around me understood.

But I felt terribly weak, inexorably constrained, held down by what no longer felt like my own choices. Nothing made sense. I hurt from the inside out, like I'd never hurt before.

My rational mind came dashing in to save the day. There must be a connection between these odd feelings and the initiation. I begged for power and got weakness? Surely I could reason this out. Surely I could apply some kind of carefully leveraged tai chi move and come out on top here.

But as soon as the wrestling match between my intellect and raw feelings began, it became clear that my rational mind was no match for the overwhelming sensations of fear and powerlessness that were defining my reality. I laid my head back down against the stiff bag I called a pillow and surrendered in defeat. Separated from home, family, and my familiar cultural milieu, completely isolated, I had nowhere to go but inward as I wrestled myself to sleep.

The next morning the eggs were cold and the tea was warm. I sat erect in my breakfast chair wondering how I would function. Ama Bombo peered across the breakfast table and touched me with her gaze, smiling like a proud parent. I was to go off to the Festival of the Cows—a day of release.

The gods welcomed me with weather that fit my psyche—it poured all day as Tibetan stick dancers clicked and shouted their way down muddy streets. Beneath my pain, I had a deep knowing that everything was just as it should be, following some grand order. Eventually back in my room, I once again fought myself to sleep after a very long, hard, heavy day.

The Return of the Eyes of a Shaman

I was excited that we were going to make a special trip to see Wang Chuk, a legendary shaman who came over the mountains from Tibet with the Dalai Lama. Wang Chuk was sick with tuberculosis, so we were unsure if we would get to see him, and I was slightly concerned about the risk of being exposed. At the last minute the trip came through and I released most of my concerns and became excited about the adventure.

Despite having been bedridden for quite a while, and virtually on his way out, Wang Chuk rose from his small bed while his assistant reluctantly adorned him with his headdress and a full assortment of sacred items. At his feet lay a strange, ancient-looking instrument that I was told was some sort of breathing machine. His soft chants began, interrupted with occasional deep crusty barks. I thought he might keel over right in front of us, and as I looked at the concern in his assistant's eyes, it felt as if that might not be far off from the truth.

His chants gradually became more and more clear, as did the echoes from his throat. After perhaps a half hour of chanting and calling the spirits, he began to shake and the bells that hung around his shoulders started to ring—indicating the spirits had entered. For the next hour and a half Wang Chuk had the energy of a forty-year-old. Watching him give healings was mesmerizing. I decided to be patient and not push my way into line, but rather just watch him work.

And then I looked into his eyes—*the bird at the waterfall*—the same unmistakable visage of the eyes of the man I had seen in the vision.

I thought he might wink at me or make eye contact, but he never did. Still, I knew somehow that these were the eyes of the shaman I had seen back on St. John and the eyes of the large bird. It is said that in the depths of the evening, in a deep and mysterious way, the soul of a shaman can travel away from their body without any awareness on the shaman's part. Although it took me many years to understand what happened in this Wang Chuk encounter, I finally became comfortable due to my own experience with the notion that he may in fact have actually visited me without my being conscious of it.

In any case, from my perspective, there was no doubt that I really had seen the eyes of a shaman.

Remember the eighteen-month-old infant who for the first time recognizes himself in the mirror as being his own body, himself, really something? At that point, he can wave his hands and know that he is the one who waved back. This was similar, except it was the magical interconnected nature of reality itself that had waved back to me and validated itself through Wang Chuk's eyes—through the eyes of a shaman—now on multiple occasions.

This was an undeniable sign, and in some mysterious way that I could not explain, in the midst of the impoverished Tibetan refugee camp on the other side of the world, I felt I had come home.

An Early Return to Search for My Heritage

The next morning, I became aware of the familiar stench once again as the sun flashed its relentless eye on my face. I was back! I broke into a silly grin as I sat up in bed. I felt as if I could run for miles, write a book, heal the world. You see, *I had been shown the eyes of a shaman!*

My newfound power began to dance with my old definition of myself, and suddenly my breath quickened as I thought about returning home and resuming my worldly responsibilities. But I still had a week to go. Today was the day I was scheduled to see Shaman Ram, the diminutive shaman whom I had briefly spoken with the first day.

This was my last of several sessions with various shamans throughout the duration of the initiation program. Despite the exultation I felt upon rising, I realized then that I was tired and just wanted to go home. I gave myself a pep talk: *Almost done; you can do this.*

I arrived ten minutes early and sat outside the door in the small hallway. Next to me was a small plate of food left over from the night before, and I breathed in the familiar smells of curry and saffron. Dr. Larry was also to accompany me for this last healing session. He was late and I was wondering if he'd show up on time. I centered my mind on the present and called in my spirit guides to help me receive everything this shaman had to offer.

"I am here to move deeper into my power so I can give back," I told the shaman.

He did not understand a word I said, as his translator remained silent. My lanky American legs were folded in a difficult seated yoga pose, and I wondered how I could possibly hold that position for the entirety of the session. I was still tired from the formal initiation, and all I really wanted was to lie down.

"My power, my reason for being here in this life—" I begin to say to the translator.

He quickly responded on behalf of Shaman Ram: "Sit up straight! Shaman Ram wants you to sit up straight, to be strong and not hide."

I realized I didn't have to speak Nepalese for Shaman Ram to see my poisons, to see what troubled me. I came fully present, experiencing the ruddy animal smell of the rope incense that smoldered among the red, green, yellow, and orange powders and flowers of the altar at our feet.

I did my very best to give this tiny man, this shaman who barely reached the height of my rib cage and who wears the same brown clothes each day, the respect he deserves. Shaman Ram continued rocking back and forth, chanting, offering prayers to the gods as I attempted to stay present with my straight back and crossed legs aching.

It seemed like an hour had passed, as sweat began to fall from my forehead and underarms, and my upper back began feeling like it was burning from the inside out. Shaman Ram's chants were getting louder, but he had still not looked directly at me. It seemed to me that another thirty minutes had passed, and since I knew that a lot of other people were waiting to see Shaman Ram after me, I calculated that I wouldn't have to hold my sitting position much longer. I can do it, I can do it, I thought to myself. In my mind arose fantasies of just lying down in front of him, but doing it so naturally that he would accept it and not find it disrespectful.

Suddenly, Shaman Ram began to shake and scream. The translator said: "He says you are a true shaman, but you are not in your power—how dare you! You are not in your power, and you have not honored your heritage. You are a true shaman, and all shamans have shamans in their bloodline and heritage. But you have not honored your heritage. How dare you not be in your power? How dare you not be in your power? Go home each day and honor your heritage, honor your bloodlines."

He and his spirits had seen that I had a similar gift to his own—but I was wasting mine. And having a gift—a real gift—and not sharing it fully with the world was the ultimate sin. He—and his spirits—were infuriated.

My body filled with chills as Shaman Ram, and then in echo his translator, shouted at me over and over again to go home each day and honor my heritage. Shaman Ram's directive resonated on a deep soul level, and I knew, in an instant, the deeper meaning of what was being said to me. Indeed, I had not honored my heritage. I was adopted and didn't know my heritage. I knew in that moment that I was being called to my next pilgrimage.

Dr. Larry tried to talk me out of going home four days early: "We will be going to Kali's temple, and she is your Goddess, so you can't go home yet!"

But I knew what I had to do. Shortly thereafter I headed to the airline office, and soon after that, I found myself back in my St. John home ready to uncover my heritage, ready to find out where I had come from so I could move fully into my power.

Waking in the Third Season—Breakthrough 7

The third season—the season of waking—can be, and by definition often is, unbelievably challenging in its initial stages. Your own third season obstacles will be uniquely suited to you, individually customized, as it were, based on your DNA, your karma, the particular needs of your soul, and the fortuities of chance. (In a later chapter I'll cover how all these factors fit together.)

If, then, as you move past waking onto a pilgrimage of initiation, don't be surprised if what you are going through looks like nothing else you have ever seen or heard. As Joseph Campbell once wrote: "You enter the forest at the darkest point, where there is no path."

For me to live whole, I had to follow my own pathway back to the beginning of this lifetime, and that meant finding, encountering, understanding, and absorbing the lessons that would come from my own unique birth mother.

The Third Season: Illuminating the Initiations of the Dark Night of the Soul

The experiences you have when you are hopelessly lost in a dark wood—when you are enmeshed in a dark night of the soul, and perhaps even suicidal—are often best thought of as Initiations. The value of Initiations was well known in the ancient world, even if today we dismiss such things as primitive. In our modern world, if the pain and darkness you are experiencing is thought to have no social utility, you are told to suck it up and get over it—pronto. And when people tell you that you're broken or that there's something wrong with you, it may be hard not to believe them.

If you happen to be in the third season right now, I want you to know that while you can accept society's version of what is happening to you—while you can buy into a cultural dream of meaninglessness and despair—there is another option. In this other option, you see and understand the value of what you're going through, you find a way to be less attached to your pain, and you move through all of it while staying awake to it. Doing so transforms the experience over time, and drastically changes the outcomes when you get past the Initiation and come out the other end, into the Fourth Season.

Realistically speaking, of course, when you're lost in a dark wood, when you're at your worst and not even sure the sun will rise the next day, it's hard to be inspired, to focus on the reason you're here, or to even believe that you're here for a reason in the first place. If you happen to be suicidal, my greatest hope is that you can feel—right now—the ancient wisdom of the shamans, guides, spirits, angels, ancestors, your inner calling of your soul, whispering to you, helping you understand that you are in the middle of an initiation, and providing you with a glimpse of a better fourth season so you decide to stay.

Bottom line: in this moment of greatest darkness, with you at your worst, context can make a huge difference. Even if it doesn't help you to feel better in real time, knowing (or even having just heard) that you're here for a reason—even if you don't know what that reason is—and that the initiation you are experiencing is designed to help you understand and get in tune with that reason, can be enormously helpful.

Having such context can help you discover your purpose, reinforce your determination, and provide meaning for what you're going through by reminding you of your deepest connections to yourself, family, and the world. Context can inspire you to accept that you are part of the big puzzle, and that by aligning yourself with why you are here, you can become capable of helping not just yourself, but the whole world. When you are at your very lowest, by stepping back and experiencing the context of what is happening, you can rapidly embrace the very highest aspects of your nature and begin to fully feel into your destiny and purpose.

I really do understand. When you are in the thick of it, the words you just read may sound like New Age babble or some flashy motivational speech. I know. But do your best to stick with me, with us, even if it is only with an ounce of what-if. Because coming through the other side is so worth making it through this side that you may be on right now. And we need you.

Finding My Birth Mother

Upon my return to St. John, I was laser focused on my next pilgrimage to establishing my heritage and finding my birth mother. This penultimate step on my journey into power was full of incredible stories and magical events that, as they unfolded, brought me ever closer to the "thing" that was ultimately holding me back, as Shaman Ram had ordered me in Nepal. This thing, whatever it was, felt like an anchor around my neck that prevented me from running full speed ahead into a truly passionate life of service and presence.

Even before my summons from Shaman Ram to find my birth mother, I had always felt called to find her so I could say thank you for giving birth to me. But finding her was not easy.

I hired a search agency that was familiar with how to proceed in these situations. After months of searching, they let me know I should prepare myself. When it was this difficult to find someone, it might be because the person was living in a nursing home somewhere or sick with cancer, Alzheimer's, or some other kind of degenerative physical or cognitive disease.

I was driven to find her and began to search on my own with the pieces of information that were slowly coming in from the search agency. Each evening I would call a list of women with the last names that matched my mother's records in the state of Florida. I would introduce myself and say I was looking for someone who would understand the significance of my birthday, and then I would provide them with the day and year.

It was such a heartfelt journey filled with anticipation and the love for some of these elderly women that were sharp enough to put two and two together to understand what I was looking for. Some of these women said they wished they were my mother, while others became my cheerleaders sending me prayers and words of encouragement on my journey to find my birth mother. In the end I missed my goal of finding her before her birthday.

The following week the search agency called me with her ex-husband's phone number because in the end it was all they could find. They also told me she might be on her deathbed, so I knew if I ever wanted to contact her, I had to move fast. But I didn't want to divulge anything about her to this ex-husband or hurt her in any way by divulging this secret, so with the adoption agency's help, I settled on a story. The ex-husband was direct and cold when I called him; he said she was in a home and gave me her daughter's phone number.

I had some trepidation about calling; it felt like a big decision, so I slept on it. But knowing she was in a home and not well, I decided to go ahead and call her daughter, that is, my sister.

"Robin, this is Lawrence Ford. You don't know who I am, and this might be one of the strangest calls you'll ever get, and I just want to make sure that you're in a place that's okay to talk." She said she was, and I told her that I was 99 percent certain that her mother was also my mother.

First there was dead silence on the other end of the phone. Then she started laughing and said, "That's stokin'! That's so cool!" She was thrilled to learn that she had a brother and let me know that she would talk to our mom and see if she was open to talking to me or even seeing me.

The following couple days felt like weeks. When my sister Robin got back to me with the news that her mom was indeed willing to see me, I was relieved. Her name was Suzie, and she had indeed been ill and in a nursing facility but was now back home. Robin arranged a call for us to talk.

I headed off to see her a few weeks later, and after getting off the plane in Florida, I drove to her place. Since I lived on a small island and Google Maps was not a very useful option in those days, I didn't know if I'd find her living in a mansion, a trailer, or who knows what.

I found myself wondering about who my birth mother was. I thought back to some of those late nights as a child, dreaming about who she might be, whether she was rich or poor, famous or nice, and so on. I found myself watching my mind—

stalking my thoughts and feelings—and preparing myself for the meeting.

I drove down a long fenced-in area and saw that she lived in a massive complex of mobile homes. I pulled over gazing at the sea of white tin box-like dwellings and experienced the cosmic karmic joke, the humility of knowing that my birth mother was not well off, with all the ego lessons that were attached to that. I took a few breaths, drove to her trailer, knocked twice, and she reached over and held me tight as tears ran down her face saying "God bless you" and "thank you, God, thank you, God," over and over again.

It was a small and simple trailer home. As I stepped up into the home, I felt the floor shake under my weight as a sour smell of day-old beer and stale smoke lingered from the ashtray on the plastic-covered kitchen table. My birth mother was sweet, her gentle loving soul shone through her piercing greenish blue eyes as she stared at me with an unwavering gaze, but it was becoming rapidly clear that she had had a tough life.

We had a wonderful time talking, and I took her out to lunch. We sat and talked for a few hours, and as she told me about my father, a man named Bill Kelly who lived in Boston, I smiled and laughed at the humor of trying to find a Bill Kelly in Boston. I said I guessed I would never find him, as there must be hundreds of men with that name in Boston.

After the visit, I flew home to St John. There, I decided to ask my birth mother if she wanted to come spend some time on the island with me. She accepted. I don't think she had visited more than a few states in her lifetime, and she had probably never gone overseas and was excited at the prospect.

A Shaman's Touch in the Family Bloodline

A few weeks later I flew her to St. John. She came for two weeks and wanted me to call her Mom. This was difficult to do, but knowing she would appreciate it, I did my best.

About three days into her visit I realized she had a serious alcohol addiction. I started thinking about hiding alcohol bottles from her and found myself getting angry. "Ten more days of this," I groused to no one in particular, "and I don't even really know who this lady is and I am being thrown into this situation, and while I've dealt with many clients with addictive conditions, I've never had a family member that was an alcoholic."

It was another thing entirely to be sharing space with someone who had an active addiction—especially when that person was a stranger called Mom. I was confused, unsure of how things would turn out or how bad they might get. I felt lost.

A little later on we were sitting on the porch when she took my hand and said, "Lawrence, I have something I want to tell you, and it may sound a little weird."

I'm thinking, "Here it comes," and I said, "Okay, what is it?"

"I think it's important for you to know that I have a gift, a little strange one, which is the ability to heal people through my hands."

I smiled inside. If she only knew! I felt a wave of emotions. First, there was a feeling of pride—perhaps she did have this gift, and perhaps I also had some of it in my blood. I felt a bit like a long-lost member of *The Sound of Music's* von Trapp family finally figuring out why he was a musician. If Shaman Ram—who had sent me back to find and honor my heritage—only knew! (Perhaps he did.)

But then, a moment later, instead of rejoicing that I had learned about my heritage, I found myself thinking, How dare you have a healing gift but you're too lost to use it? How dare you not be in your power? I did have great love and compassion for her and kept my feelings contained, but I became so angry and sad at such a waste of a special gift, as well as the loss of her own joy in this life for not embracing it.

How could she have a gift like this and squander it away? How could she be killing herself with booze instead of using this gift? Then I felt a pit in the bottom of my stomach as I flashed back to Shaman Ram yelling at me about not being in my power, how I could have a gift like this and not fully use it to give back to others. The karmic collision hit me deeply, and I saw the beauty in the lesson I was receiving.

Still angry and confused, we packed up to go to my girlfriend's home for dinner. "We" included my kids. A month or so earlier my teenage daughter had stepped on a rusty nail and had to be flown to a mainland hospital because she had developed osteomyelitis, an incredibly painful blood infection in the bone near where she had stepped on the nail. She was treated successfully and had been back on the island for a few weeks.

Laughter filled the home as the evening ritual of the sun tucking itself to sleep behind the mountain redirected the evening breeze into the open windows lifting the smell of island cooking through the room.

My daughter said, "Daddy, it hurts really bad."

I responded, "What do you mean it hurts really bad? Do we need to get you back to a hospital? On a scale of one to ten, how bad?"

"Daddy, it's like a nine." She had tears in her eyes, and I was thinking we'll have to fly her back to the mainland the next day and somehow get my birth mother home as well, and my stomach sank.

Then my mind turned: My birth mother is here, and she's troubled, but also a healer, right? At that point I was skeptical about her supposed healing ability (despite my own similar experiences) and was losing some patience with her. I was frustrated on so many levels, and this seemed like a good way to take out my anger by proving that this fantasy of her being some kind of healer—along with the whole gift-in-the-bloodline thing—could be disproved in a public setting and put to rest once and for all.

So I asked my birth mother if she'd go see how my daughter was and maybe help her.

"Is she okay?" my birth mother asked.

"No, she's in terrible pain."

She went to my daughter and asked me if I'd mind if she put her hands on her.

My rational mind was thinking she was full of it, but I found myself saying, "Yes, go ahead and see what you can do." Basically, part of me was hoping she would prove that I was right and that she was a fraud.

I watched out of the corner of my eye, pretending I was looking at something else while she did her own kind of hands-on healing ritual. It looked like a traditional religious prayer, and she said a good deal about Jesus and God and how it was through them that her hands were able to do healing.

After a while she finished up and headed toward the kitchen. I casually sauntered over to my daughter who looked absolutely terrified. I assumed that all of the praying might have freaked her out a bit, although such things were certainly not foreign to her. She was about fourteen at this point and relatively worldly and mature.

"Honey," I said to her, "what's wrong?"

"Daddy, I'm scared."

"Why are you scared?"

"Well, Daddy, it's gone."

"What do you mean it's gone?"

"The pain," she said. "All of it. It's just … gone."

I felt a rush of mixed emotions and thoughts. Perhaps my daughter was delirious. Maybe the timing of her feeling better was just a pure coincidence.

But as I settled down, my feelings once again turned positive, even exultant. I now knew my mom's abilities were undeniably real, and that my gift might not be so strange after all. I was experiencing events that were beyond my belief and beyond my understanding of what was possible. Perhaps I had found my heritage with its hidden gifts. Or perhaps I was just somehow evolving and beginning to see and feel things that I had previously been blind to.

Following my mom's visit, it became clear to me that my time in the Caribbean would soon be over. My ex-wife and I had a continual and acrimonious custody battle, and eventually I realized I needed to be back on the mainland full-time and focus on giving my kids a stable home. My new partner, now my wife, agreed to come back with me and start our own life together away from the islands. She had two kids of her own, a boy and a girl who were best friends with my own kids and exactly the same ages. I had secretly always wanted a big family, and the four together looked so happy. I had pursued my dream of a healing center, and now it was time to move on.

A couple years after returning to a big town in Connecticut from my tiny little island in the Caribbean, I found myself confronted with some more press, including a talented and highly professional journalist named Laura Blumenfeld from the *Washington Post* who found me while I was living in the islands and was now writing another article about me, this time as a cover story titled "The Shaman of Wall Street."

I was writing my book, this book, raising my now four incredible children with my beautiful wife and struggling to find myself in a world that seemed insane with its greed, wealth disparities, degradation of the earth, and crashing stock markets. It was becoming increasingly difficult for me to find my feet in this once familiar land.

Following undeniable signs, I decided (or perhaps just surrendered) to do the thing I once thought I would never do: I was guided to launch another wealth management firm, to *be* the change I wanted to see in the world of money and personal empowerment. I would bring together consciousness and capital, helping people to live their dreams by aligning their investments with their values and lead this company with a loving, supportive environment in an industry filled with so much fear and greed.

In other words, I was simply trying to be myself. That meant figuring out how to fit who I really was into the current worldview that surrounded me, while also addressing all of my (and my family's) everyday worldly concerns. Many days it was tough. The markets had crashed. I had lost nearly all my savings in the divorce, and I found myself starting over with four kids, each a few years away from college, with another child on the way.

And then it started to happen.

My Numb-er Was Up

> ❝ And then the day came when the pain it took to remain tight in a bud was more than the pain it took to blossom.
>
> —Anaïs Nin

Two of my daughters were starting out at college. One flew down to Florida, but I was able to drop the other off at her Rhode Island school. I was carrying some of her belongings up the stairs and suddenly there was a terrible numbness throughout my whole right side. It was like half my body was gone.

If you've ever watched yourself on a closed-circuit video screen, you may have experienced moving your arm, followed by a delay, followed by seeing your arm move on the screen. That's what it was like, with my whole side numb. Nervous and quite frightened, I managed to keep my condition to myself because I didn't want to ruin my daughter's first-day-of-college experience.

Please, let me just get out of here so I don't wreck this special day, I thought. When the day was done, I went to a nearby emergency room. They checked me out and said they didn't see anything wrong, and I felt a bit better.

About a week later, in a shopping mall, it happened again: My whole right side went terrifyingly numb. I figured I was having a stroke, so I told my fiancé Yvette (later my wife) that she needed to drive me to the hospital. Yvette, and the three kids that were still living at home at the time, hopped into the minivan and in near silence we drove to the emergency entrance.

By the time I got to the trauma room, lying down on a stretcher with bright lights assaulting my eyes, I couldn't talk or move. They handed me little pieces of paper so I could scribble down what was going on with me, but even that was too much.

I had literally been reduced to the functioning ability of an infant. My mind worked—sort of—but I was frightened and didn't know what was going on. All I could think was that I was having a stroke. Finally, they gave me some medication and I fell asleep.

I woke up the next morning and saw my parents (my adoptive mother and father who raised me and loved me through all seasons and whom I consider to be my true parents) sitting next to me.

Then spirit spoke to me in my mind, and I heard these words: "You can't do it this way anymore."

I found myself internally protesting—to whom, exactly, I wasn't sure: "Are you serious? After all that's been happening to me, is that *all* you're going to give me now?" I wanted more—usable—clues as to what I needed to do, not a nebulous question that didn't point me in any particular direction.

I was to find out, in my own time, that this message was the result of the download I received. At that time I was only capable of understanding the essence of the message—that we can't do it like this anymore—that the world needs a new perspective and approach. The teachings had sunk into my bones—the message was the secret of the seasons and the beginnings of a new operating system behind it—but it would take me time to sort things out over the next seven years and learn how to communicate what I had experienced.

Throughout that day several doctors and interns came by to interview me and ask questions about my health and the level of stress in my life. It seemed to me they were all nodding and metaphorically winking to each other about the executive who worked too hard, the high-functioning male who has had a little breakdown. The resulting plan, of course, was to give me some medicine and send me home. Their overall attitude, driven by conventional medical thinking, was helpful but condescending and clearly was missing the overall big picture.

I didn't take any medicine, but instead just went home and seemed to get better. And indeed, I did get better, and for a while it seemed like nothing had ever happened.

A couple of weeks later, on a Sunday, I went to a local Frisbee golf course for the first time. It was just a normal low-key weekend, and I figured I'd go out and play some Frisbee by myself, which was atypical of me because I was almost always working or helping out at home with family and house matters on the weekends.

All the holes on a Frisbee golf course are marked, and I was heading up a hill to the next hole when the numbness began to hit me again. I sat down for a minute, thinking how odd it is to be at a little Asian-looking pagoda out in the middle of this park in the middle of Connecticut, and saying "Gee, please don't do this to me again," while trying to pretend that there was nothing wrong with me.

I got up and then had some trouble finding my car—I was lost in the woods. I took a shortcut that ended up being the longest route I could have taken because my car was just a few hundred yards behind me. By the time I got to the car, my right arm would not work at all.

I began driving home, shifting the car into drive with my left arm, weaving in and out, driving like I was drunk. I managed to get back home safely, but I'm not sure how.

A Perfectly Arranged Breakthrough

" Dis-ease of the mind, body, or spirit is merely a growth bump on the road to power. It is a gift as long as one is willing to open the package.

Arriving home, I immediately told my partner Yvette that it happened again. But I felt strongly that it was not a medical issue but, rather, a spiritual one. I also told Yvette that there was one person that I could think of who might be able to help me. Sheryl was her name, and she was in effect an ancient wisdom holder posing as a therapist, someone whom I had never seen professionally but had come to know of by her reputation.

I had Yvette call her, and she happened to be home and picked up the phone. We drove to her home where she also had her office. The numbness was getting worse, and as we entered her office, I saw the fear in both of their eyes. Sheryl and Yvette felt I might be better served by going to the hospital, and by the time I arrived, the numbness was the worst it had ever been.

I found myself uncomfortably waiting in a little spot in the emergency room, surrounded by other people suffering a wide range of more ordinary maladies. I literally felt as if I could not stay in my own skin. It was like I was being ripped apart from the inside out. I must have looked like a mad man to everyone around me in the waiting room. What was happening to me would have made complete sense from a shamanic worldview back in Nepal, but to Western medical science, it made no sense at all.

I should clarify that while the numbness was not that different from what I had experienced the first couple of times, the feeling of being torn apart—of being ripped apart from the inside out—was by far the worst I'd ever experienced. I desperately wanted to run away, to jettison myself from my body to avoid what was happening, but, of course, that was not an option.

And then an odd thing happened. Apparently, the only word that came out of my mouth was *drugs*, presumably because the last time I'd gone to the hospital the only relief I got was from some medication they'd given me. Yvette and Sheryl were there, desperately explaining—in an effort to defend me—that I was a high-functioning type of executive male and not a drug addict.

Despite their efforts to defend my character, the lack of empathy from the medical attendees was decreasing along with my condition. They tied me down to a stretcher as they asked me probing questions about my life habits. This forced me to reexperience what it felt like to be an infant who is overpowered and rendered helpless. From this perfectly reenacted infantile state—with nowhere to go, and no place to hide, and being overpowered with no physical means of defense—I was forced to face my deepest fears and soul's wound.

In that situation—tied down and reduced to nearly zero functionality and ability to communicate—I realized something very important: I was not afraid of dying. Sure, I wanted to live and spend time with my loved ones and continue to share my gifts with the world, so I wasn't in a rush, but the realization that I was not afraid of dying was decisive.

What I was terrified of was that I would become a burden to my family, an out-of-control victim who had nothing to offer anyone, a helpless and useless adult who no longer could care for and control his environment. And that fear, of course, brought me right back to the core soul wound that was aching to be retrieved. I laid there tied down to a gurney. I erupted with waves of pain and discomfort that hurt so badly I floated in and out of consciousness while I experienced a perfectly orchestrated drama reliving the exact same feelings of powerlessness I'd had as a helpless infant—as preparation for eventually being reunited with that missing piece of who I was.

Put differently, here in this moment in my third season, in the deepest darkest of woods, I felt I had become worse than nothing. Tied down, I couldn't move; I couldn't speak; I was forced to relive the feelings behind the atrocious abuse that had happened to me in the first six months of my life. The pain of abandonment and unconscionable treatment I had experienced in foster homes as an infant was beginning to boil through my veins.

Everything I previously thought I was—everything that defined me—was being dismembered by the spirits, broken apart from everything that had held me together for forty-something years.

At some point I was blessed with passing out. I was told they eventually gave me medication, which aided in this blessing. When I woke up the next day, I felt somewhat better. For the next few days I remained in the hospital going through a presidential-level checkup. Naturally, they couldn't find anything physiologically or organically wrong with me—I was completely physically healthy—and the recommendation was that I should probably take some time off.

Seeing and Hearing Everything

The next year consisted of a horrifically painful and exhilarating initiation beyond description. The experience was so bad there were times when I honestly did not fully believe the sun would rise the next morning. And I'm not using those words to be cute or for dramatic effect. I really did come to a place where I did not fully believe the sun would rise the next day.

Physically, I was soon well again, with the numbness entirely gone. Internally, though, I was simultaneously gifted with feelings of hopelessness as well as states of incredible peak perception where I could literally see the spiritual big picture in front of me, in real time. My training and personal growth had allowed me to come deeper into my gifts including the ability to use the power of my mind to shift into an altered state of consciousness to work with my patients. In that state I experienced many extraordinary visions and messages to help my clients, but this was on an entirely different level and completely beyond my control.

It's difficult to find the words to describe these peak experiences because these experiences transcend the mind's ability. I could see and hear everything, both about the people I was interacting with and the natural world as I moved through it. For example, if I got on a plane or train, I knew exactly where everyone would sit, and even what they would do next. Time became bendable, and the veil of ordinary consciousness was lifted. The animal world seemed to "see me" and speak to me with stark clarity offering guidance and support. The universe was alive and part of me, and I was part of it.

For a while, I could even perceive energetic flows everywhere, in people and nature, almost like seeing the stream of numbers in the matrix and hearing animated depictions of radio waves or electromagnetic energy flying through the air. The problem was, there were periods when I was always on—I had no way to shut it off, with a huge amount of information constantly pouring through my mind and into my soul while walking through my otherwise ordinary day.

Experiencing the highs and the elevated glimpses beyond everyday reality was a test, but it was nothing compared to the darkness that began to envelope me. Previously, I had worked with hundreds of people who were depressed, but I had never known what depression felt like. Now I knew, and it was the worst feeling you could imagine—and if you can't imagine it, then count your blessings.

Every day—literally, every day—was a struggle for me to be in my own skin. But despite my depressed state, life went on. I was successful at hiding my tortured state, as well as my peak experiences, even from those closest to me.

From the lows of my state of being, I now better understand the state of shock people feel when someone close to them takes their life and they didn't even see the signs. Because mental health is so misunderstood in our society, the stigma of feeling depressed is matched only by the extreme shame of being seen in this kind of state. And it is because of this shame that when people are feeling like life is no longer worth living, it is often worse to admit that you feel this way than it is to die.

Life and work continued as I flew around the country, speaking to top banks and independent broker dealers—I even worked with a Nobel Prize winner for about a year—while also continuing to see individuals for investment and empowerment work.

A Last Visit with My Birth Mother

During this period, from time to time I reached out to my teachers for help.

My birth mother became very sick, so I flew down to Florida where she was now in a nursing home room that was basically serving as a hospice. Since she wasn't smoking or drinking there, we were able to have some good conversations, and while she didn't let herself fully open up, a few insights became clear to me.

My birth mom didn't want to talk to me about what happened to me when I was a baby, or even why she did not keep me. (Later on I came to know that I had been abused so badly that I nearly died.)

I also learned that my blood sister—the one I originally contacted to find my mom—had a twin brother, as well as uncles and cousins who were beautiful people. I had time to get to know my sister, who is really a good person, and was proud of everything she had become despite her challenged upbringing. My brother, on the other hand, seemed not to have fared as well and was living in the streets. I send him blessings each day knowing that could easily have been me.

Seeing my birth mother on her deathbed, I was able to thank her for all she had done for me. I am reminded of a quote: "Just because someone doesn't love you the way you want them to doesn't mean they don't love you with all they have." We had a nice few days together. I told her that I expected her to stay in touch after she was gone, and she smiled.

Later on, when she had passed, I went to her small funeral and burial. I blew my conch shell three times to bless her and guide her with safe passage as she moved into another dimension. (Guiding the deceased soul with safe passage as it transitions into its season passing on—known by the Greeks as *psychopomp* work—is a traditional function of many shamans.)

A few days later my birth sister sent me an astonishing picture of an angel-like form that appeared in the back of a picture of her and her son. It was so clear, it looked like one of those pictures you see of ghosts that you are certain must be doctored to make them look real. But there was no doctoring here, and I was sure it was my birth mother saying hi. And honoring the deal we made at her burial ceremony.

Soul Retrieval on My Birthday

My big breakthrough came literally—not by chance—on my forty-eighth birthday.

My adult body was finally ready to process the fear that had surreptitiously coursed through my veins since my infant preverbal trauma. I completely broke down and cried like a baby for maybe an hour and a half, releasing ages of pain and suffering. I released the preverbal trauma that I had gone through as an infant and released an extraordinary amount of pain and old stuck energy. I was in the midst of my soul retrieval.

I figured it was time to give back to myself what I had shared with so many others. A few days later I performed my own soul retrieval ceremony, based on what I had been taught in Nepal and had guided many others through. A few days later the symptoms disappeared—like someone turning off a light switch—with the depression never to return again. Thank God.

By the end of the week, I had put all the pieces fully together and knew with certainty that the dynamic that had kept me running for forty-eight years—the experience that dismembered me, ripped me apart, reduced me to my core, opened me up, and forced me to face my deepest soul wound—was now healed. I was moving into the fourth season, the season of living whole. I was now ready to fulfill my reason for being here. I was ready to stand in my power, walking in two worlds at once.

But reentry was going to introduce its own worldly challenges.

The Four Sea Sons: A Parable of the Four Seasons

Four Sea Sons were born to the God of the Sea.

The First Sea Son, who never grew older than eighteen months, was always so blissful because without fail he knew the purity of his soul and the depth of the universe's love for him.

The Second Sea Son became a man of the world, from which he naturally tried to derive his identity by trying to be really something. In the end, he failed because it was an impossible task.

The Third Sea Son was very close to the Second Sea Son, but eventually found himself lost and alone, surrounded by darkness. Not knowing what to do, he fell back asleep to numb his pain.

The Fourth and last Sea Son had been in the dark with the third but found his own way out. He remembered that he was indeed the son of a God, but he also knew that he was here to be in the world, and do good things, and so remained in both worlds at once.

The Fourth Season and the Soul System Operating Map

8

In this chapter, we'll first consider a little bit more about what it's like to enter into the fourth season. Then we will put it all together and give you the soul system operating map. Then in the next chapter I'll discuss what it's been like for me to be in my fourth season, before turning to pragmatic steps you can take to manage your own waking dream as powerfully and effectively as possible.

Like the swan that fumbles with an awkward gait as it works its way to the water's edge, finding your own ground, your true element, in the fourth season requires a period of getting ugly and awkward. Once you have found your element and taken the courage to let go, like the swan nervously letting himself down into the water, life shifts and you are carried forward like the majestic swan gently rolling over the waves. Often the best things are beyond description but words like *flow, non-*

dual awareness, Wu Wei, the *Tao*, *grace*, all point in the right direction to describe this state of being.

[Note: Remember that the seasons are not linear. You can be in the fourth season of living whole for a short or long period of time and then find yourself engaged in second season activities or find yourself going through another cycle of third season waking, from darkness to light, from despair to hope, from fear to love.]

Not only is the process a trans-verbal or trans-linguistic state or understanding, but each of us experiences our own fourth season quite differently. On top of that, even within the fourth season as any of us individually experience it, there will be ebbs and flows of their own distinct character and nature.

If you are in the fourth season right now, or can remember a time when you were, you may very well be able to feel—or remember back to feeling—the interconnectedness of all life, knowledge, and power. You may not be able to control much of that equation, but you may to some extent be able to see it, feel it, know it, and, over time, become part of it.

While the fourth season is about as magical and powerful a state of being as can be imagined, it is not a place of narcissistic egoic absorption or elitist self-satisfaction. Quite the opposite: when you are living whole in the fourth season, what is normally thought of as the ego fades.

Moreover, despite what you may have heard from any number of self-proclaimed enlightened teachers, this is not a perpetually positive state of butterflies, kittens, and rainbows. When you are awake, dancing with eyes wide open in the midst of everything, you see all the beauty, wonder, and magic—as well as the context of how you fit in personally—but you also see all of the pain and all of the loss. Even when fully woke in the fourth season, mystery always remains, and deeper understanding always awaits.

A New Operating System for Living Whole

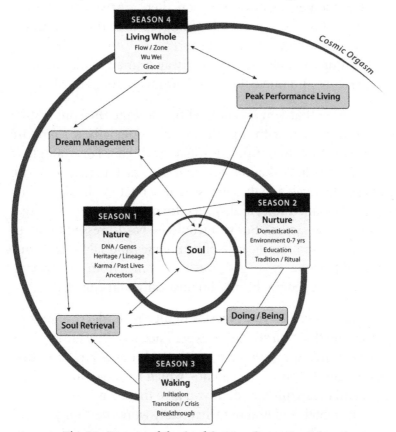

The Big Picture of the Soul System Operating Map.

Now let us look at the soul system operating map—the whole picture—of our lives and the guidance we are always receiving—whether or not we are aware of it. A major premise (and purpose) of this book is that if you have the big picture in your mind—even if you've seen it and experienced it just once—it will provide you with the kind of context that will make your life easier and better regardless of the season you are in right now or are transitioning into.

Moreover, when you look at the soul system operating map, if it seems somewhat obvious to you, there are two good reasons for that. First, we've been building up to it throughout the entire book and, second, it represents—more or less—the way things actually are and the way human beings actually experience and move through their incarnational realities.

Also, note that you should feel free to take the soul system operating map with a grain of salt, especially if there are elements that do not fully resonate with you. For example, if you don't believe that the personal deep factors that comprise us as individuals and that are listed under nature should include past lives, ancestors, and spirits, then that's just fine—forget about those factors. But you would be hard-pressed to doubt the reality and significance of your genes and DNA, and your overall personal heritage—everyone comes from somewhere, biologically, geographically, linguistically, and culturally.

Similarly, even if you have difficulty in understanding or accepting that everything we experience while we are awake is part of a living dream, many of the techniques and tools that fall under dream management—which I will get to shortly—will still bear fruit for you if you give them a go. Be open, be experimental, and find out what really works best for you and those people, animals, environments, and organizations you care most about.

Before actually walking you through the soul system operating map, let me make just a few other points. First, you'll note that the underlying or organizing principle is a spiral. One of the fun aspects about spirals is that while they are circular or round in nature, they bring you back to a similar point, not the same point, along a path. If you walk through a spiral rock garden, you will get a similar but different vantage of the rocks and trees from each similar but different point around another turn of the spiral.

As you move through the spiral, starting with birth in the center, you are moving forward, through a kind of energetic path or structural formulation that many, many other people have already gone through. You are building to living whole in the fourth season, and in a certain sense, we are all building forward to the final season—to the season of moving on—which is not part of this particular soul system operating map, but which I'll get back to in a little while.

Finally, you will note the Cosmic Orgasm at the top of the spiral. This indicates that in some sense the entire universe—the very ground of being—is generated by an unfathomable act of creation of the universe experiencing and loving itself. The spiral pathway we move through as human beings unfolds as the universe embraces itself and enacts its own self-knowledge. This is the big aha! The ultimate orgasm of life, the cosmic joke.

The Soul System Operating Map: Winding Our Way through the Spiral of Life

And then the next particle/wave of humanity happens, and I encourage you to refer to the map itself as you read about each season here.

Season 1 – Being

Flowering from the universe's inexhaustible creativity, a soul becomes inextricably interwoven with a human body—some say as early as conception, but certainly no later than birth itself.

Upon birth, that soul finds itself in the center of the soul system operating map, at the beginning of the first season of being. It then spirals up and over, greatly influenced by and pulled by its nature, as constituted by the personal deep factors this particular human being came here with. These factors include

- Trans-generational epigenetic inheritance,
- Our DNA and genes,
- Our heritage and lineage—we all come from somewhere,
- Our past lives (if these are real and can be usefully accessed),
- Our ancestors and spirits (which I personally believe everyone is attended by), and
- Everything else we came into this life with.

At first this soul, this person, experiences only pure being—knows itself only as a soul—and for most of the next eighteen months or so, it is mainly occupied by and with the dynamics of being. At some point, however, the second season—the season of doing—starts to beckon each human being and calls upon them to start synching up with the outside world. Moving down, around, and then up, this human being is not solely shaped and formed by the personal deep factors of its nature, but over time is increasingly molded by nurture's environmental impacts and the domestication process that we all go through.

Nurture's environmental impacts—the demands that it makes and the directions that it pulls us in—can be more easily understood through the lens of psychologist Abraham Maslow's famous hierarchy of needs. Beginning at the start of the first season, our deep physiological needs for air, water, food, warmth, and sleep are paramount. But soon, as we begin heading toward the second season, other needs become more prominent: our need for touch and belongingness, for being sweetly held, loved, and personally nurtured.

Season 2 – Doing

Eventually, as we begin to interface with the outside world and those not from our immediate family or household, we begin to experience higher developmental needs for esteem, prestige, and accomplishment.

Maslow's hierarchy, of course, ascends even further and ultimately includes both fulfilling one's full potential and evolving into what Maslow called self-actualized individuals who were both completely fulfilled and doing everything they were capable of. But, of course, as we wind our way upward in the spiral, we could not experience the bounties of our full potential and Maslow's self-actualization while we are still in the second season.

Season 3– Waking

Instead, a crisis of one form or another inevitably reared its head and we found ourselves first moving into and through the third season, the season of waking, with any luck on our way to the fourth season of living whole.

How this all unfolds, and whether we move back from season three into season two before we eventually come to season four, is a matter of individual chance, what some might call karma, kismet, or destiny. (The spiral shape of the soul system operating map as drawn here lends itself to thinking of the children's game Chutes and Ladders: At any moment you can slide down into a previous state or climb up to the next highest level.)

Some of us will experience relatively light crises as we move into season three and then naturally, spontaneously, find ourselves unfolding into the living whole of the fourth season. Others will struggle, will go through one or more truly horrific dark nights of the soul, and will require various kinds of help and assistance. Some of us—perhaps many of us—will require, as I did, a full-on crisis and soul retrieval, whether undertaken by a shaman, a psychotherapist, or a trained guide.

The third season isn't easy, and it isn't meant to be easy. If you helped a butterfly pupa out of its cocoon, it would die—not even fly—because you robbed it of its struggle, its process. Our doing, in the midst of a crazy world, takes us so far afield from our being that typically only a powerful set of shocks and readjustments can break through and remind us of our more natural condition. And some of us may in fact never make it through season three and into season four. Death, depression, mental illness—all these can effectively sideline someone throughout the entire spiral of life.

Season 4 – Living Whole

The good news is that now that you are familiar with the soul system operating map, you are much more likely to have the contextual wherewithal to eventually find yourself living whole in the fourth season—a compass in the dark wood. Even better news: the various tools and techniques discussed throughout this book, like stalking, like leaning into your heliotropic soul, and like engaging the conscious dream management tools and alternative operating system focused on in the next chapter will greatly increase your odds of fully and completely synchronizing your life with your reason for being here as you enter into your own fourth season.

The big picture context, the new operating system, and the specific dream management tools I'll soon get to will make a tremendous difference in how you, personally, move through the seasons, and whether you emerge into your own fourth season and can give the fullest flowering of your gifts.

My hope is that both the four seasons generally, and the soul system operating map walk-through of the seasons, will provide you with a similar sort of overview effect. The big picture overview of human existence—how we come in, our struggles, our triumphs, our skills, our faults, our tragedies—boggles the mind, opens the heart, and makes our sense of curiosity yearn with wonder and fascination. Let it open you up, reorient you, and help you ever more fully engage with your reason for being here.

Taking Advantage of a New Operating System and the Conscious Dream Machine

Taken together, the soul system operating map and the basic principles and practices of shamans and other ancient wisdom keepers, described earlier, provide us with the beginnings of a new operating system, a blueprint or set of instructions for how our individual experience and realities are co-created. Having already gone through the general parameters of this new operating system, we will now consider some methods or exercises for better operating it or perhaps operating within it.

That is, how can we better move through the seasons by taking advantage of how reality is actually constructed? How can we use the incredible innate abilities and toolset of the human being to take advantage—in the best sense possible—of what has already been afforded to us? Where do we start, what is important to focus on, and how do we make sure we get results?

Putting the Operating System into Action

Let's quickly take it from the top.

The big picture taken in conjunction with the practices and principles that arise from a magical interconnected universe provides us with a new operating system, a new way to live. There may be dangers in using the current scientific norms as a model for explaining things. Freud's psychology model, for instance, is based on hydrodynamic flows of steam and water, like in a steam engine, but given the detrimentally ratcheting-up prevalence of computers and technology in our lives, this seems like a good place to start.

The new operating system starts with the precept (just as does ancient Hindu philosophy) that in many instances mind comes before or is causally interconnected with matter, and that by holding a solid image—a dream—of what you truly want in your mind and heart, it is more likely to come true. The principles of visualization are ubiquitous in business and sports because they work. Exactly how they work is not so clear, but that they work cannot be doubted.

One place to start is with a dream map, a visual illustration of your dreams, kind of like a vision board. Much has been written about how to put together a dream map, but, in truth, you can do it however you like. But there are some basic principles you should consider following based on the many years of success experienced by myself and my clients:

- Use specific images, ideally ones that you search out on Google Images and then print out or cut out from magazines, including images that you draw on or change digitally or make collages out of.

- Don't be afraid to overstate what you want in your dream map (without putting out something that's physically or otherwise impossible to obtain or attain). It's only meant for you, and you must be willing to really put it out there to the universe if you want results.

- You can use some words, either handwritten or cut from magazines or printed out, but don't use too many.

- Don't focus on too many things. Over time, experience shows that the maximum number of dreams to focus on at one time is about five.

- Be experimental and daring. If you've never visited some place, don't be afraid to put it down, or if you've never taken a certain type of course or tried a certain type of activity, lay it out for yourself to see and make real.

- When you feel you have reached a stopping point, step back and look at your dream map and see how it makes you feel. If it doesn't make you feel happy, excited, enthusiastic, and alive, then keep working with it for a while.

- Make sure you look at your dream map regularly, ideally at least once a day at the same time, and give the whole map some time and focus as well as practicing the two exercises we're about to come to.

- Above all, remember that your dream map is designed as a GPS to help guide you in a positive framework as you practice aligning your doing with your being, so paradoxically it is not about attaining the dreams that you put on your map, it is the journey that is the success.

My daughter Sage began doing dream maps with me when she was six. One of the images she had on her map that first year was a picture of a large cruise ship floating through a tropical background. That summer her older brothers and sisters came for a visit, and we all went to Newport, Rhode Island, for a day-trip.

A silly little water taxi held twenty or so people and brought its passengers to various ports within a couple miles or so. We decided to hop on to just enjoy the short journey, with no destination in mind. Sage sat on my lap on the bench seat on the starboard side rail. It was an open vessel, and the breeze blew through her hair as she hung her hand out to touch the water.

Her toothless smile was interrupted as she turned to me and whispered: "Daddy, I did it!"

"Did what honey?" I responded.

"The cruise! The one on my dream map! I made it real."

I thought about the line I once heard from Saki Santorelli: "Kids are like parachuted-in little Zen masters."

In her beautiful wisdom and innocence, Sage was able to let go of the conditioned details of how big the boat was supposed to be or that the background was supposed to include palm trees, but instead had the wisdom to embrace the essence of what she was looking to accomplish on her dream map.

So stay awake and let the magic of the universe and soul's longing guide you. Since, as Einstein said, "No problem can be solved by the same consciousness that created it," it may by that definition be impossible for you to know exactly where you want to go, because as you go, with an awakened second season intent, you will be shown possibilities that you were not conscious of when you began the journey. Let yourself be surprised as you let go of the small consciousness and domestication that you were bound to before you left the shore.

During my speaking and leadership trainings for individuals and corporations, I outline some of these practices in detail. One is called Will/Want/Welcome and another Think/Feel/Be that actuate the new operating system. They cannot be covered in detail in this volume, but will be made available over time, either online, in speaking and training events, or in a follow-up book. For more up-to-date information please see www.LawrenceFord.org.

> The power of waking is the gift of showing up to this experience called life and becoming an active dreamer and co-creator of your intended destiny.

Summary of Lessons in Principles 9

Each season has at least one secret or principal lesson. More precisely, each of the four seasons has a primary secret or principle, and then the time of moving on or death—that also has a secret. Finally, from a slightly different angle, wrapping around all of these secrets and principles and tying them together is the power of waking.

When do the secrets come into play and how do we work with them?

The soul system operating map (from chapter 8) shows us all of life in just one image. It gives context and a way of beginning to see or understand everything all at once. But even in its simplest form—which brings together nature and nurture, the four seasons, the underlying spiral that we all wend our way through, and encounters with crisis, the dark night of the soul, and even the need for soul retrieval—the operating system is complex. If you are in a crisis, or just happy or in a quiet reflective moment where thinking more than necessary is unappealing, then that is a good time to turn to and work with one of the secrets.

Similarly, the new operating system and conscious dream map laid out in the last chapter describe a way of seeing and working with reality that can powerfully impact nearly all aspects of our life as well as our collective experience. But you do have to practice with the tools and techniques that are suggested, which involves slowing down, bringing your imagination to bear, and focusing your willpower.

Each of the secrets is simple, in that the secret itself can be expressed in a few pages or paragraphs. But of great potential value in the sense that the overall concept of the four seasons alone can change your life—and the lives of those you touch— in a spectacular fashion that brings to bear the power of your own reason for being here. A life that wakes you up to a new relationship with a living, responsive universe that ultimately wants nothing more than for you to succeed beyond your wildest expectations.

You can think of these secrets or principles, then, as being a type of repetitive phrase, prayer, or mantra that you come to know fully within your own being. In good times and bad, they will help you relax, see what is really before you, and tune into the necessary right path of action. Bring them with you wherever you go like a lucky stone in your pocket.

Ultimately, *secret* may be the wrong word, because to the degree the information embodied in these secrets is part of the legacy of universal wisdom traditions, these secrets have long been known and available to at least a select few. But now it's time to more broadly offer these secrets to all who are awake and ready to hear and embrace them.

The Secret of the First Season (Being)

The first season is the season of being. When we are born into this world, we know—before words—that we are a soul. We know without any question or doubt that we are pure and that we are both an expression of pure love and fully loved by the universe.

The simple secret of the first season, then, is that each of us doesn't just have, but is, a pure beloved soul. That is, early in our lives, each and every one of us has experienced— beyond any doubt or questioning—the pure love at the heart of existence that is our very birthright.

If we seek love—and who among us does not seek love?— then what we seek is already part of what is seeking. This also means that at any time—at any moment, in any season, facing any kind of difficulty—you can remember the love that you once experienced because ultimately you still *are* that same love. The saving grace of your very own soul is eternal, and you should never hesitate to reach out to it, especially in times of greatest despair and trial.

The light of your soul, the love of your heart, and the truth of your being are all ultimately on call because that is who you always were, always are, and always will be.

The Secret of the Second Season (Doing)

The second season is the season of doing and often lasts through a large portion of our life. In the second season we attempt to align our being with our doing. In this process, we inevitably come up against a world that is not designed to allow the flowering of who we are and why we are here.

While this dissonance—this mismatch between who we really are and what we are expected to do and initially try to do—is a positive and necessary part of the path, it can cause great upset along the way. But still, we would not experience such dissonance and its emotional impacts if there wasn't something even deeper attempting to push through and direct us. Our natural direction and efforts—what Aristotle called our entelechy (for example, the entelechy of an acorn is to become an oak)—are what drive the problems that inevitably rise.

What this means, then, is that we *do* have an entelechy. **The simple secret of the second season, then, is that each and every one of us has a reason for being here.** You are not just here by accident. Instead, you are given a complement of gifts and tools that are precisely tailored to your deepest soul urgings and the gifts you were meant to bring through and give to the world.

The second season can be difficult, but if you know deep in your heart that you have a reason for being here, these difficulties will lighten and not only become less burdensome but can be seen as a gift.

The Secret of the Third Season (Waking)

The third season is the season of waking. Movement into this season is often—perhaps usually—precipitated by some kind of crisis during the second season and may involve moving into and through a dark night of the soul. It may also necessitate a soul retrieval to facilitate a full healing of the person involved.

My own soul retrieval, relating to what happened to me as a small child, was highly unique and particular to my needs and experiences, in accordance with how the personal deep factors of my nature encountered and were transformed by my difficult early experiences.

This kind of uniqueness also applies to the crises and difficulties that are the hallmarks of the third season. These crises and difficulties are once again both unique to each person and often extremely difficult for that person to go through, perhaps the most physically, emotionally, or otherwise painful and distraught period they have ever experienced.

And while you can appreciate and empathize with the intensity of someone else's experience and pain, you're unlikely to ever truly know what they are experiencing on a qualitative level.

After the fact—looking back at the growth that was spurred, the healings that came about, and the new life paths that coalesced into greater levels of health, happiness, and productivity—these hard times and challenges begin to take on a different light.

Not only does it become clear that traversing the hard times was absolutely necessary, but without doing so, health, healing, and greater prosperity would not have been possible. **The simple secret of the third season, then, is that initiations are ultimately extraordinarily valuable wake-up calls that precipitate fully aligning our doing with our being and moving into living whole in the fourth season.**

Put differently, the secret of the third season is that the most difficult times and crises you will ever face are actually, in computer lingo, features and not bugs, structural elements designed to help you move into full alignment with your reason for being here.

The Secret of the Fourth Season (Living Whole)

When you are living whole, moving in and as a state of non-effortful flow, all of the other secrets and the soul system operating map and principles of ancient wisdom are both obviously true and completely unimportant. It's just the way things are and how you are when you are being who you really are and doing what you are really meant to be doing.

The secret of the fourth season, of course, is that ultimately there are no secrets. There are still mysteries in the universe, inside and outside of us, and throughout all of nature and the cosmos, but that which was secreted away—that which was purposefully hidden—is revealed to our deeper sensibilities when we are living whole in the fourth season. What used to be secret, then, becomes obvious to us in an interconnected magical universe conspiring to help all of us live a whole life of purpose.

Pragmatically, what this means is that when you are living whole in the fourth season, you are not trying to find a hidden reason or purpose, a secret final answer or explanation of the meaning of life, that will finally make you happy. You're already happy. You already have everything you could need or want.

The Time of Moving On (Death)

This is the time of passing, of death, ideally, of moving on with dignity. But if you were hoping that the message of this time would be a fact or truth about what happens when we die that your mind can know with absolute certainty, then you will be disappointed.

Why? Death is unknowable. The human mind is simply not fully capable of understanding death, and if given free rein, the mind can and will dysfunctionally fixate on that which it cannot understand. **The simple final message of the time of moving on is, then, to not seek knowledge of death with your mind, but to feel into it with your heart, intuition, and body if you wish to gain insight and live whole.**

Another way to think of it is that the time of moving on represents the quintessence or quintessential distillation of the most essential elements and dynamics of the previous four seasons. In this sense, we can expect death to be like the other seasons, somehow structurally and energetically formed by where the other seasons have led us. This season is further along the spiral path of life, yes, but it is still on that spiral, and where it leads us is still part of the path we're on and have been on.

Many if not most people, at some point in their lives, find themselves actively fearing death.

Death, I now understand in a full-bodied way, is just another reality transition, another dream. While we are alive, our souls live within a kind of reality bubble co-created and held together by the joint efforts of our minds and bodies. This reality bubble is something we have to work hard at holding together. Simply by reading these words, you are already doing a lot of work.

Put differently, it's a tremendous blessing—but also takes a lot of work—to be a conscious human being. Since the natural state of matter is to move to disorder, holding together so much energy and matter effectively reverses entropy. Given how much negentropic effort being and staying alive takes, it's no wonder that death beckons to some as being wonderfully exhilarating. I liken it to carrying heavy bags of groceries up a flight of stairs. You don't really know how much energy you were exerting until you put the bags down.

What happens when a human life ends? Let's continue with the premise that life itself is not what we think it is. In effect, life is really just a waking dream, and when that dream ends, it's like turning another page in a book, moving from one chapter to the next. The waking dream known as life, however, can be experienced as a true nightmare if we don't realize that we are in a dream—something we can't rationally know. Again, we can't use our mind to figure this out. True knowledge comes not from the mind, but from experiences—in this world and others—that transcend ordinary knowing.

In addition, I have been blessed to have experienced my journey from a life and then back. As mentioned before, the mind cannot know, but let me share my direct experience with my own death and rebirth—a re-membering that I was blessed to experience one early evening with the guidance of a fellow shaman.

I saw myself leave this body and watched two people from that life sitting beside me as I left my physical body. I ascended, I felt all my human fears and joys pass through me like a gust of wind on a crisp fall day. I met with my "soul group" and was returned to the edge to begin my reentry. Leaving was hard but I was told it was to be.

As I began my journey back, I fell into this confusing mix of knowing everything and not knowing anything. I was being taught the ways of the dream of the land I was about to reenter as I simultaneously left an all-knowing state of unbridled light. As I made my final tumble through the tubes coating me with sticky mass, my lessons, I was told, would be fast and brief as I landed in my birth mother's belly.

So while I don't know the left-brained details, I have complete faith in my understanding of how death and life relate from my own personal experience, as well as from observing many clients with past life experiences, and communicating with many souls that have passed that appear when I am working with a client and they come to help.

I may not know if time goes backward or forward, or if time exists at all or instead everything happens at once. But what I do know is that when we die, we release all of this energy that we have been using to hold ourselves together in our current form, and we go back to our core soul state, the primordial unbridled energy of our being. Thus, the essence of Lawrence Ford will continue after my death. Not Lawrence Ford, as you know him. But his/my essence, his/my soul.

Thus, I have no fear of death, because I know—beyond what my mind may challenge—that death is not the end. I wish this for you.

We have already said that a soul is a unique vibrational frequency, resonance, song, or pattern, like a snowflake, that is individually unique to who we are. Has every one of us, through our souls, been here before? Perhaps.

I have encountered hundreds of people who appear to have existed in other times and places that to them are as real as their existence in today's world. Many times during my sessions, my clients recount fascinating rationally minded inexplicable experiences that suggest past lives. Again, my mind can't completely understand or make sense of these experiences, but my inner knowing and personal experience says that they are very real.

The Power of Waking

All of us—every single human being—possess the power of waking. It goes to the very core of who you are as a divine, aware being—one with the potential to wake up at any time, in any moment, and then increasingly return to that aware state.

Like Dorothy clicking the heels of her slippers, there is a ruby-pure magical current—a cascading spiraling vortex of infinite quantum entanglements—that not only runs through you, but actually *is* you.

That's why at any moment you can return to your experience of yourself in the first season as a pure soul.

And that's also why, in the subsequent seasons, at any moment you can exercise your capability and capacity to align your soul with your destiny—to align who you are with what you are meant to do, and to feel and experience joy and know you matter—so that there is no longer any distinction between how you are living your life, moment by moment, both in your thoughts and in your actions, and how you are benefiting and blessing the rest of the world and those in it.

The simple power of waking, then, is that it is always present within you and you can access it and begin living whole at any moment. The power of waking is not a special gift that only a few possess or exercise, or that is meant for members of only certain nations, religions, or ethnicities. It is not reserved for dedicated spiritual seekers or guarded by secrets that take a lifetime to decode.

Moreover, the power of waking is not about the amazing sensations you may feel and experience once you begin to consciously move through the seasons or use to arrive in the fourth season of living whole. Put differently, the power of waking is the gift of truly showing up to this experience called life and becoming an active dreamer and co-creator of your intended destiny.

So while you actually are a magical being, healer, and reality co-creating soul—a generator of miracles—what's most important about the power of waking is that at any moment you are completely capable of waking up to your destiny and contributing your personal genius and divine calling to a world that desperately needs you to be all of who you are and become fully in synch with your reason for being here. You are built to bridge this world and the spirit world, and to give your gift so fully that you cannot but help benefit everyone and everything that you encounter. You are here to achieve your birthright and weave your perfect thread into the tapestry of life.

And the necessary abilities and capabilities needed to wake— those are a built-in part of who you are from the beginning. Once you know the secret—that the power of waking is always available to you—you may find yourself accomplishing many things that you previously had not thought possible. And as you make more use of the power of waking, it will remind everyone around you that they, too, have this built-in blessing.

So go click your heels and say:

I'm here for a reason

I'm here for a reason

I'm here for a reason

… and the world needs me!

Individual and Collective Co-Creation of Our Best Possible Futures

10

> *Our consciousness determines our perspectives,*
> *our values, and our behavior. Consciousness and*
> *capital are the two most powerful forces on earth.*

The belief that we individually don't matter and that we cannot make a difference is the greatest travesty of our time.

Every human being's soul sings a song unique to his or her own being, and each one of us makes a difference. When our *being* is out of alignment with our *doing*, that unique blissful and blessed soul song becomes rapidly and painfully out of tune, and we begin to think we don't matter. And when we, as a species, collectively sing out of tune, each of our souls contributes to the deafening chorus like ten thousand fingernails scratching on ten thousand blackboards, making us feel as though there is nothing we can do to change the trajectory of individual or collective discord.

With the collective song so terribly out of tune, we begin killing each other in the name of religion and ideology; we abuse whatever power (political or otherwise) we may possess; and capitalism is allowed and even encouraged to run amuck, with some of the worst elements of human behavior being lauded and extolled. If we stay on this course, we may (and likely will!) drive our species—and at this rate perhaps most earthly life—to extinction.

Despite the recent calls for global action like the Sustainable Development Goals helped developed by United Nations and agreed to by 193 member states, we find ourselves in a terrible place of inaction. We are experiencing a mild disgust, but not quite uncomfortable enough to initiate complete transformation, so we do just enough to keep things interesting by unconsciously repeating dysfunctional behaviors while the tides rise.

Wake-Up Calls Come to All

Fortunately, in accordance with the seasons, third season wake-up calls also come to families, organizations, corporations, nations, and the world as a whole. In fact as I write this book, we are all together experiencing a global third season that is beckoning us to come together en masse and raise our consciousness to overcome the destruction of our home, planet Earth, during the outbreak of a global pandemic. As part of my reason for being here, I have done what I can to design this book as a wake-up call and guide to living whole so that others can hear a dream that I have long held, which is this:

One day we will realize that there is nothing more important in the world than knowing that each of us has a gift and that we are all here to support each other to live that gift. We are here for a reason.

Soul Medicine

This book is designed as soul medicine at a critical time for our species. Why do we need soul medicine? Let me quickly tell you one final story.

I was required to come back to the hospital about six months after the numbing wake-up began in my body for an obligatory meeting with the neurologist in charge of my case. He had his head down in a clipboard, asking me routine questions, when I finally called him by his first name—it's a good trick to get a doctor to actually make eye contact with you—and told him that I had just one question for him.

"Jim, this thing that happened to me, have you ever seen anything like it before, ever?"

He looked up at me, and what he said sent shivers through my body—and still does: "All the time. It happens all the time."

In that moment, I felt as if I had barely made it through the darkness myself with all of the experience helping hundreds of people through their transitions, and my training and support by some of the wisest sages in the world, and if it was true that so many other people were experiencing similar symptoms, I knew I was to write a book that would give people some context when they were going through similar experiences and to remind each of us we are here for a reason.

Context

In a world where materialistic reductionism seems to be winning out, having context is critical. In addition to whatever context you may have gained, for example, by reading about the heliotropic soul or working through the soul system operating map of the four seasons, it's critical that you remember everything you've already experienced, including who you ultimately are. And if you can hold to your reason for being here, and allow signs and hot spots to guide you, then there is little that can ultimately hold you back.

If all else fails, remember to occasionally slow way down—even stop completely—and become fully present. Your own radiant ground of being and connection with the universe is always available to you.

Remember: on the deepest level, you are love, you are connected to everyone and everything, and you are here for a reason, a unique purpose and manifold destiny that has always been yours and only yours to unfold. Your entelechy—your designed, perfected final condition—is yours alone, and you have (like Dorothy in the *Wizard of Oz*, always had) everything you need to achieve it.

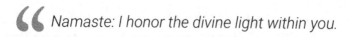 *Namaste: I honor the divine light within you.*

The power of the nexus of consciousness and capital—

Even as we have fallen asleep—even as we have abused nature, our planet, and our very ground of being, even as a global pandemic is upon us—a deep inherent ecological connection with the earth and each other has spoken to many of us. As we become aware—as we are, in effect, forced to wake up and listen—we experience a kind of wisdom that is different from the matter-of-fact knowledge about "how to do things" that is the received wisdom that has been demonstrated to us throughout our lives.

Unfortunately, our powerful minds and our willingness to accept the atrocities we now see everywhere have collectively brought us to a dangerous place. Our minds are predisposed to a kind of self-worship, a mental narcissism pervading the realms of politics and power, which in turn leads to aggressive, thoughtless, destructive behavior in nearly every realm of human behavior.

We find ourselves consumed with taking sides, with using our personal stories—our dreams—to fight against each other: nation against nation, Democrats vs. Republicans, socialists vs. capitalists, black vs. white, my religion vs. your religion. And on it goes.

What we are missing is the awareness of the gift of the third season being offered right now, beckoning us to wake up from our slumber, reminding us that we are all one and are all called to come together to redirect the trajectory of our species while there is still time. During this time of waking we can begin to heal the connective tissue between consciousness and capital, our species' two most powerful tools.

Acknowledgments

I never understood why writers drone on about who they are grateful for until—

Jordan Gruber. This book could have said on the cover, *with Jordan Gruber*, and in truth this book would not have been possible without Jordan Gruber. Thank you, Jordan. Your craft is at the highest level and your patience and dedication to this book is what made it possible.

Gene Stone, a master best-selling author and my literary zen master, thank you for demanding that my writing be real and true in every sense of the word. To Martha Hills who helped me edit my first piece down in St. John and reminded me to call myself a writer far before I was worthy of such a title.

To Susanne Davis, a professor of writing and accomplished author, who taught me the art of putting a story into words. To my Sunday spiritual group and friends from the islands who brought my consciousness game to a new level. To my students who bring me so much joy and humility as I watch your transformations and courage through all seasons.

To Sandalar, kali, Tak Nang, David Chandler, Will Kennedy, Dorothy Martin-Neville, Julianna, my petty tyrants, my dear friend and teacher Ama Bombo, my mothers, fathers, sisters, and my beautiful amazing kids, Lexy, Chandler, Chancie, Josh, and Sage. And to my special "real Mom" who is the most amazing mother any kid could ever dream of. And to all my relations.

To my wife, Yvette, who watched as I headed to the computer many nights to write instead of going to bed, after tucking the kids in and after a long day—and who keeps me grounded. To the selfless Heather Desjardins who is my right hand each day and who had faith in this book and pushed me when I needed it most.

To everyone else I didn't mention, you know who you are.

About the Author

Lawrence Ford is the CEO and Founder of Conscious Capital Wealth Management and the Founder and Chairman of Future Capital. He has had a long, admirable career as an entrepreneur, financial advisor, consultant, coach, author, speaker, and spiritual leader.

He has dedicated much of his life to being a bridge between the modern world of business and the ancient world of wisdom, which is why Ford was dubbed the "Shaman of Wall Street" by the *Washington Post*, and *The Economist* magazine referred to him as a "man of two worlds." NPR named him "The Finance Guru," and the *Retirement Income Journal* calls him "The Spiritual Advisor."

Through these two worlds, he is helping people and organizations "wake up" and remember that they are here for a reason.

As CEO of Conscious Capital Wealth Management, he helps clients align their dreams and values with their money.

Through his global leadership with the United Nations and the Sustainable Development Goals, he is the founder and chairman at Future Capital where he is convening global leaders to leverage the nexus of consciousness and capital to co-create global economies that are good for all life.

In addition, Ford offers coaching and speaking programs for individuals and corporations to help them operate at peak performance and to live their reason for being here.

For media and speaking, consulting, and coaching inquiries, contact him at www.LawrenceFord.org.
Email info@LawrenceFord.org.